CONNELLAN, Thomas K. How to improve human performance: behaviorism in business and industry. Harper & Row, 1978. 185p ill (Continuing management education series) index 77-11614. 10.95 ISBN 0-06-041349-2. C.I.P.

A comprehensive but concise review of basic behaviorism principles and their application in both business and industry. Connellan has made a commendable effort in reviewing concepts of motivation and learning, especially reinforcement, shaping, schedules of reinforcement, punishment, and extinction. Important in this work is its elucidation as to how to identify the variables and description of how they can be controlled. By giving several specific examples incorporating a wide range of situations, Connellan demonstrates how problems may be analyzed, objectives determined, and systems designed to change human behavior. The clarity of the examples is outstanding and permits the conjecture of almost limitless applications. Highly recommended for libraries whose readers are interested in influencing the behavior of others, particularly in a business setting.

How To Improve Human Performance

CONTINUING MANAGEMENT EDUCATION SERIES
Under the Advisory Editorship of Albert W. Schrader

Forthcoming Series Texts:
FINANCE FOR THE NONFINANCIAL MANAGER, Raymond Reilly
SELECTION INTERVIEWING FOR MANAGERS, Thomas Moffatt
MAKING THE TRAINING PROCESS WORK, Donald Michalak
and Edwin Yager

HOW TO IMPROVE HUMAN PERFORMANCE:
Behaviorism in Business and Industry

222201

Thomas K. Connellan

THE MANAGEMENT GROUP
ANN ARBOR, MICHIGAN

Harper & Row, Publishers

New York   Hagerstown   San Francisco   London

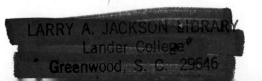

Sponsoring Editor: Laurie Ann Caplane
Project Editor: Karla B. Philip
Designer: Katrine Stevens
Production Supervisor: Stefania J. Taflinska
Compositor: Bi-Comp, Incorporated
Printer and Binder: The Maple Press Company
Art Studio: Vantage Art, Inc.

Library of Congress Cataloging in Publication Data

Connellan, Thomas K
    How to improve human performance.

    (Continuing management education series)
    Includes index.
    1. Personnel management.   2. Organizational behavior.
3. Employees, Training of.   4. Performance standards.
I. Title. II. Series.
HF5549.C719   658.3   77-11614
ISBN 0-06-041349-2

Contents

Preface

Today's manager is faced with a problem of increasing magnitude—how to best utilize the human resources of the organization. In organization after organization managers tell us that the human element is the largest single controllable variable. What this suggests is that if an organization is to maintain or improve its overall performance, it must improve the performance of individuals within the organization. This book describes the techniques involved in improving human performance. Moreover, it shows the reader how to put behavioral techniques to work as a science or a technology.

Until recently there was really nothing very scientific about the "behavioral sciences," primarily because the key elements of a technology were not present. What was missing was one or more of the following elements of a technology:

1. the ability to identify the variables that affect performance;
2. the ability to predict the changes that will result if the variables are changed;
3. the ability to change the variables;
4. the ability to repeat or duplicate the changes

This book contains techniques that meet these criteria. Behavioral technology is neither "human relations," "behavioral sciences," nor "warm feelings." It involves specific proven techniques for changing human behavior in a wide variety of organizational settings. As a management tool, behavioral technology has been around since the early 1960s—not very long when compared with other management tools, such as planning, organization, delegation, and so on. These new techniques, while perhaps requiring some necessary refinements, nevertheless give the individual manager an important new tool. Morever, behavioral technology does not replace delegation, communication, or other management skills. It is not an addition to the manager's job—it's a way of helping managers do their jobs more efficiently, a way of improving important skills, such as delegation and communication, in a scientific fashion.

Thomas K. Connellan

Acknowledgments

No book on behaviorism would be complete without acknowledging the work of B. F. Skinner. You will find his name in no other place in this book, not because his contribution to the thoughts expressed herein was so small, but because they were so great. There would be no application of behaviorism in business and industry had Skinner not developed behaviorism as a technology.

Special thanks from all who apply behaviorism in organizations must also go to Geary A. Rummler, Karen Searles Brethower, and George S. Odiorne. Geary and Karen began to develop organizational applications of behaviorism before the rest of us, and George, while director of the University of Michigan's Bureau of Industrial Relations, actively supported their efforts.

James V. McConnell contributed to the book by adding to my knowledge of behaviorism. Both Frank Petrock and Ed Pedalino have contributed to this book through their close working relationship with the author. Donn Coffee, Toni Coffee, Albert W. Schrader, Daniel Schwalbe, and Karen Brethower all aided by reading and commenting on the original manuscript.

Special thanks must go to my wife, Sandra, who endured my erratic hours during the preparation of the manuscript, who because of her professional competency and expertise was able to critique the final product, and who once upon a time helped strengthen a formerly diminished interest in behavioral technology.

Finally, to those many managers and organizations with whom I have worked in applying behavioral technology, thank you for help- ing shape the contents of this book.

T. K. C.

How To Improve
Human
Performance

1

The Performance Crisis

Today's organizations face a performance crisis. The declining performance of both private sector and public sector organizations is of increasing concern to managers, economists, and politicians—to all of us who are interested in human performance and productivity in the work setting. ▮

Some managers, however, are countering this trend. John Sweeny is one such manager. John is the general foreman on the afternoon shift at the Master Distribution Center for a major automobile manufacturer. This center covers over 1 million square feet of warehouse space and contains 105,000 different automotive parts. Between 40,000 and 60,000 line orders a week are shipped, Each day 600,000 pounds of material are moved in and out of the warehouse. Inventory runs around $50 million. John's firm is considered a well-run company.

In a three-month period, absenteeism in John's work force (excluding vacations, but including excused absences, unexcused absences, and disciplinary layoffs) fell from 9 percent to 3.6 percent; the percentage of orders filled during the course of a day increased from 80 percent to 100 percent; tickets "bounced" because of improper bin locations dropped from an average of 45 per day to an average of 5 per day; incoming loads unplaced at the end of the shift plummeted from an average of 70 per day to an average of less than 1 per day.

June was a key month for John because in that month he started applying the techniques of behavior change to his job. He attributes his successful results solely to the application of these principles; similar results have not been achieved on other shifts where the techniques are not used, nor have any other changes been made in the work situation. John is one of the new breed of managers who finds that new techniques of changing employee behavior pay off not only in improved morale among workers but also, and more importantly, in improved performance on the bottom line.

Then there is Harry Miller, one of the top salesmen for a large chemical company. He has been the top performer of its agricultural divisional sales team for a number of years. However, Harry has been somewhat of a problem to his regional sales manager. His travel and entertainment expenses have consistently been too high. A series of regional sales managers, including his present supervisor, have spoken to Harry about these expenses. The results have always been the same. Harry would agree they were too high and would promise to lower them, yet nothing would happen.

Most companies have their Harrys. Harry will not be fired because he is such a good salesman. He knows this, and as long as his expenses do not get exorbitantly out of line, he and his superiors will continue to justify the expenses because he produces. Getting tough with Harry's type doesn't do any good because it tends to damage morale and destroys the effective team relationship that has been built up between the supervisor and the employee. Moreover, although expenses may drop a bit, total job performance generally declines even more.

Interestingly, during the past four months Harry's travel and entertainment expenses have dropped 13 percent. Four months ago Harry's regional sales manager attended a workshop on the application of behavior-change techniques to job performance. Since then, he has been applying the techniques with Harry. The results are eye-opening. Harry is attacking his job with new vigor. Says Harry, "My expenses have been too high for years; I knew it and my bosses always knew it, but we never really did anything about it. This is the first time that anybody has been able to get me to cut my expenses and at the same time keep me committed to the job. We have discussed what is going on, I know what my supervisor is doing to me, I see why he is doing it, and what is more, I am enjoying every minute of it." Harry has a new-found respect for his supervisor as well as much lower sales expenses.

Howard McPherson is vice president of operations for a multimillion dollar company in the commercial and consumer grounds maintenance business. One of the reports Howard uses to make decisions is his "quality performance" report. This report gives detailed monthly breakdowns on the quality cost of doing business, including warranty, reject, rework, scrap, and inspection. Over a six-month period, Howard's staff has initiated a series of performance improvements including analysis, workshops for key employees, and implementation of performance improvement projects. Over that same six-month period, the cost of quality to the company dropped significantly: savings are running at approximately $400,000 a year.

John, Harry, and Howard are all anomalies in today's organizations, where human performance problems abound. In their own varied situations, John, Harry, and Howard counter a trend that is of increasing concern to all who are interested in human performance and productivity in organizations.

"Productivity," or "human performance improvement," means different things to different people. To workers, productivity means a speed-up in their work patterns. To union leaders, it means the opportunity to negotiate for higher wages. To management, it means increased profitability; to consumers, it means better goods at lower cost; to marketing directors, productivity improvement increases the firm's competitiveness abroad by reducing the cost of its goods sold in foreign markets; and to economists, it means an increase in our country's standard of living tied to gains in output per man-hour.

No matter who is affected when we speak of productivity or human performance improvement, the United States has lagged far behind the other major industrial nations in productivity gains. According to the U.S. Department of Labor, the United States ranks eleventh among major industrial nations in annual increase in output per man-hour of manufacturing. 2

In the long haul, economic growth can come from only two sources: (1) increased numbers of people in the labor force and (2) increases in what this labor force can produce. Unless labor productivity increases, the economy cannot provide a rising standard of living for everyone. Importantly, any increase in population unaccompanied by increased productivity could well reduce everyone's income.

Within the major industrialized nations, it is unlikely that any significant gains in productivity will arise from increases in population. With average family size diminishing, the population of the United States and other major industrial nations will at best increase slightly, probably hold about steady, and perhaps even diminish slightly. Increases in productivity then will have to result from increases in what the labor force produces in foods and services.

In examining where increases can be made in goods and services, it is necessary to turn from a macro to a micro view. Here we also find significant problems in human productivity. Consider, for example, the following:

- A recent government report entitled "Work in America"[1] notes that worker productivity is low. Among the measures cited by the report are absenteeism, turnover, wildcat strikes, sabotage, poor quality products, and reluctance by workers to commit themselves to their work tasks.
- Absenteeism and tardiness are problems of increasing magnitude in today's organization. Absenteeism alone, for example, is estimated to cost American industry in excess of $9 billion a year.
- Increasing numbers of white-collar workers have performance problems that make a significant impact on company performance. Many management experts, for example, say the real energy crisis is not in the utility plants, but in the ranks of supervisors and middle management.
- A recent Gallup poll suggests that 50 percent of all wage earners could accomplish more each day if they tried; 30 percent of the wage earners said those increases could be 20 percent or more.

This micro level of productivity should be of most concern to today's manager because he faces it daily; it affects his organization's performance; and it determines his success on the job. However, economists and government leaders should also be concerned with the micro level of productivity for they make up the macro level, which is usually measured by the output per man-hour produced.

Improvement at the micro level can come from two sources: (1) technical changes such as higher dollar investment per worker in capital goods and technological improvements in capital goods or (2) changing human behavior in organizations. Whereas increased mechanization, technological changes, and increased investment per worker in capital goods can all contribute to improved productivity, it is with changes in human behavior that the greatest payoffs exist. Between 70 percent and 80 percent of the gross national product (GNP) is paid out in some form of worker compensation; for the purposes of this discussion, let us say 75 percent. That means if we purchase a new car for $8000, $6000 of the purchase prices goes for salary or some sort of worker compensation rather than to the cost of raw materials.

Clearly, not all $6000 was spent within the automotive firm that produced the car. Some of those salary dollars were paid by the automobile manufacturer to the firm that did the tooling, and other salary dollars were paid to the firm that produced the steel for the cars. Some salary dollars were paid to the trucking company that transferred materials to the assembly plant; some were paid to the rubber company that produced the tires; some of the salary dollars were paid to the mine that produced the iron ore, as well as to numerous other suppliers of materials for the automobile. So, although the 6000 salary dollars were not all distributed within the automotive firm itself, they did go to pay someone for producing something that went into the final production of that automobile. It is with the 75 percent of those dollars that we must concern ourselves.

Worldwide business is entering a phase of diminishing returns from automation and further technological improvements. Although improvements in these areas will continue and will continue to affect productivity, real gains in productivity must come from changes in human behavior. There are no shortages of ideas on how to improve human behavior. If anything, managers are overburdened by such ideas, suggestions, and theories. What managers lack is a science, a technology, or a system to improve human behavior.

Techniques for changing human behavior exist not only in theory but also in practice; these techniques have paid off on the bottom line time and time again. Today there is only one excuse for enduring low productivity due to improper human behavior: when the cost of obtaining the desired behavior is not worth the benefits.

Joseph Schumpeter said that innovation is the only basis for survival. It is the same with the development of techniques that change human behavior and improve human performance on the job. This book focuses on innovative techniques for changing human behavior.

To understand where we are today, it is helpful to take a short trip backward to see where we have been—not to dig up artifacts regarding human performance, but to gain perspective on the situation today. Improving human performance in organizations by definition includes something we call "work." Barry Posner, W. Alan Randolph, and Max S. Wortman, Jr., have provided some interesting observations on the role of work in society. They suggest that there are nine different stages that indicate the evolution of the role of work in different societies:

1. Primitive culture makes little distinction between work time and free time. In fact, many languages of primitive peoples used the same word for "work" and "play." The majority of these peoples' time was spent providing for basic needs.

2. Ancient civilizations—Egyptians, Greeks, Romans, and Incas—believed work to be a curse. Work was regarded as manual labor to be performed by slaves. Individuals fortunate enough not to be slaves were expected to study the sciences, liberal arts, and physical culture. Distinctions between work and nonwork activities began to emerge during these ancient civilizations.

3. Early Christianity placed a positive value on work not only as a means of gaining wealth (to share with the poor), but also as a way of avoiding idleness, which was taught to be responsible for evil thoughts. The early Christians directed their energies toward the organization of the church and viewed this direction of energies as an instrument of purification and attainment.

4. Medieval Christianity (primarily in the form of Roman Catholicism) suggested that work was good because it was painful, humiliating, and a remedy for temptations of the flesh. As long as work conformed to the plan organized by God, it became the duty of all. However, work was given a moral goal (charity, for instance) because the church could not allow work to become an end in itself.

5. The revolution that accompanied the Reformation of the sixteenth century, on the other hand, gave work an intrinsic value. Martin Luther maintained that work was the base of society and made no distinction between religious work and other types of work as long as they both were done in obedience to God. Work was regarded no longer as only punishment for sins, but, more importantly, as a God-given opportunity for people to be creative and establish a new way of life.

6. The new economic order brought about by industrial revolution was accompanied by an almost insatiable demand for

workers. There was dramatic increase in the number of legitimate callings, or occupations. Accumulation of the benefits of one's work became a measure not only of a person's piety, but also a mark of cleverness, skill, and creativity.

7. Twentieth-century America further separated the concept of work from religious doctrine and accorded work special status. The importance of work was dramatized during the development of the labor movement. During the days of the Great Depression, "having a job" became a major obsession. It was generally felt that the work an individual did not only contributed to his fellow beings but made one a better person simply by virtue of working.[2]

Today, that work ethic has, for the most part, disappeared. Employees come in late or not at all. Rework and scrap rates go up at the same time output decreases. Yet, "profits" underlie the very basis of our economic social system. The decrease in performance has led to a decrease in profits. As a share of the gross national product, after-tax profits in the 25-year period from 1950 to 1975 have declined from almost 9 percent to less than 5 percent. Curiously enough, this decline in profits has come at a time when increasing numbers of people are complaining that corporations are "ripping off" the public with "excessive profits." Major opinion polls in recent years have shown that individuals estimated the average manufacturing profits of firms at an excess of 30 percent of sales, when actually these figures are closer to 5 percent. People question not only work, but also the value of working.[4] More importantly, they question the whole economic system under which work is performed. Capitalism, in whatever form, is questioned and attacked from all sides. "Profits" has become a four-letter word. It is no wonder that confusion exists as to the amount of profits earned by individuals and firms. Basically, confusion exists as to just what profits are. As can be seen in Figure 1.1 profits are simply the excess of output over input. They are the value added by the process in which the organization is engaged. Whereas we commonly think of profit as dollars, in the true economic sense of the word, profit is the value added to the materials and time that goes into the organizational process. Profit has been expressed in such diverse ways as bushels of corn per acre, barrels of oil pumped, or tons of coal mined.

Although the word "profit" has generally been reserved for business organizations in the private sector, it might well be argued that public sector organizations—colleges, governments, and hospitals—may show a profit just as business organizations do.

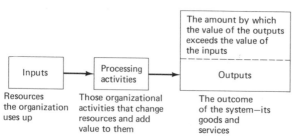

FIGURE 1.1   **Excess value of outputs over inputs**

Business profits show up on the organization's bottom line as earnings per share, but "profit" in a university might take a different form; for example, increased knowledge and skills of graduates. A hospital shows a "profit" in the form of improved patient care as well as reduced costs; a government unit shows a "profit" in the form of improved services or increased operating efficiency.

Thus, the issue is not profit versus nonprofit, but the form of profit. Utilizing the basic definition of profit as the excess of output over input or value added in the organizational process, we can see that all organizations should have some profit and should return more to the economy in value than they are using up in resources.

Whatever form profit takes, there are several very important reasons for profits. Profits are needed to create excess funds for the development of new technologies or for the rearrangement of old technologies. Profits in the health care field have led to the development of new methods of treating cancer, hemophilia, and renal disease; of improving dialysis machines and open-heart transplant surgery; and of providing new operating room equipment. All these results are from profits in the health care field.

A miner with hand tools can produce an average of three tons of coal a day. Equipped with power tools, he can produce as much as 10 tons a shift, and with fully mechanized equipment, he can produce as much as 50 tons of coal per day. In all these cases, whether health care, mining technology, or automobile production, it is profit that has not only inspired people to develop the necessary machines and technologies, but more importantly, profit has provided the capital necessary to produce these new technologies. Although the role of new technologies in improving organizational performance is diminishing, it is nevertheless an important one and it is only through profits that such development can continue.

Profit is an important guide in decision making. Profit is the feedback that tells decision makers whether or not the goods and services being produced are meeting the consumers' needs. Profit acts as a sort of compass giving the organizational ship something to steer by so it remains on course. Even though temporary deviations in a good course occur often, they will not usually occur for very long periods. Witness, for example, the disastrous experience of the Ford Motor Company with its Edsel. Its profit picture told Ford pretty quickly that the Edsel was not the car to produce; the profit picture provided vivid evidence for the company to use in deciding to discontinue the Edsel.

Profit provides an important tax base for government at all levels. Municipalities, state governments, and the federal government rely heavily on corporate taxes. These taxes are a form of transfer payment from the individual consumer to the government, but they are nevertheless an important part of our tax base and would not exist if corporations were not able to turn a profit. One might question the amount and allocation of taxes, but we are not concerned with that here. The question is do we need a government and does that government need taxes. The answer to both those questions is "yes," which in turn makes profit essential.

One reason individuals have the incentive to develop new products or provide new services is the dollar profit that can be obtained by introducing something new into the marketplace. Both psychological and monetary satisfaction accrue to individuals who introduce new products successfully. Furthermore, although we usually consider economic satisfaction the primary motivation for introducing new products, conversations with heads of companies and examination of case histories show that psychological satisfaction is, in many instances, almost as important as monetary satisfaction. However, in a market economy typical of most Western countries, the monetary return from the introduction of a new product or service provides a measure of how successful that product is. If the introducer of that product or service is looking for psychological satisfaction, it is many times to the monetary return from the product that he must look to determine his psychological satisfaction, for only that return determines how successful the product has been in the marketplace.

Finally, profits provide for a recognition of individual differences and creativity that would not be possible under another economic system. Each of us has unique desires, wants, and ambitions and on either a personal or organizational level, profits allow us to pursue these individual desires by providing flexibility in our decision-making process. One way of looking at this notion is to regard each purchase that we make as a "vote" for the manufacturer of the particular product we purchased. Everyday is election day for the American consumer; for only those manufacturers who are able to satisfy the consumer can make a profit and continue in business. The free enterprise system is remarkably responsive to individual desires and needs. Not only are individual needs met, but more importantly, people can meet those needs creatively. Each individual can "vote" for a combination of goods and services that is unique and meets a particular set of needs. Thus, by selecting items that meet our individual needs, each of us can purchase a slightly different package for ourselves.

With profit making at the heart of the economic system and human performance a key determinant of profit, three possible changes could be made to solve our current performance crisis:

1. We could change our economy to some other system that might improve human performance and thus profits. In theory, this might appear laudable. In practice, however, it does not seem to work well. History shows us many attempts to form economic systems in which all members share equally. Few of these systems survive for any length of time. Our own Pilgrim Colony founded in 1620 was based on agreement that all members would share equally. Since there was no individual reward, there was no individual incentive and less and less was produced each day. Finally, famine riddled the community and the system was abolished by mutual consent in 1623. Curiously enough, this was replaced by a private enterprise system that provided not equal shares but equal opportunity to profit through individual effort.

The Bolsheviks in Russia at the outset proposed a society in which all men were paid equally for their work and factory output was directed by workers. Profits from plants were distributed by the state in support of long-term objectives. By 1921, however, productivity had dropped to the point where a new economic policy was needed desperately. Pay differentials were once again adopted and managers were installed in plants to direct the efforts of workers. Lenin explained that this new policy was "urgently necessary to increase labor productivity, to abolish deficits, and to assure profitability in every factory." It is clear that the Communists used the profit system. The difference was (and is) that the profits accrued to the state and not to the individual.

Even this modified form of profit system has its problems. The Soviet Union now permits collective farmers to cultivate small private plots in their spare time and to sell the produce for their own profit. Although these plots account for a mere 4 percent of the land under cultivation in the USSR, by value they produce 25 percent of the country's food.

2. A second alternative solution to the current performance crisis is to remove legislative and collective bargaining barriers to improve human performance. Such barriers, according to one trade magazine, include the prohibition of labor-saving machines and devices; the requirement of unnecessary work or of duplication of work and of excessive nonproductive periods or downtime; the limitation of employee workload that restricts the number of machines a worker can operate; the requiring of unneeded workers; the restriction of duties of workers. This is a good alternative and one that is needed, but agreement on it and its implementation is a long way away and anticipated results are still further away.

3. A third alternative is simply to change those human behaviors that will lead to improved performance. Techniques exist that do change employee behavior both dramatically and permanently. We will examine these techniques throughout this book.

2

Systems Theory and Human Performance

Most businesses at the beginning of the twentieth century were relatively small. Their operations were simple, even simplistic, by today's standards. As a result, little or no thought was given to something we could call management, let alone a system of management. The closest these businesses came to a system was the owner-manager making a mistake, correcting it, and vowing never to make it again. Experience was the best teacher. Although there are no data to support this assumption, it is safe to say that experience was often a harsh teacher. It usually gives the test before it gives the lesson. At any rate, the business organization at that time was usually a few employees supervised by the owner-manager (who was also usually performing many of the technical tasks himself); the company had few products, few transactions, and not a very large dollar volume.

Following the period of the owner-manager type of organization came an era when the economy was built upon mass production/mass consumption. Different operations within an organization were broken down so simply that novices could learn a job with little or no effort. Specialization, division of labor, and emphasis upon high-speed machines required vast new pools of manpower from which to draw. From the farmlands of America came droves of potential workers who had been displaced by mechanization on the farm and who were used to working long, hard hours. As fast as this labor pool was used up, it was replaced by even larger numbers of first generation immigrants equally used to long hours and hard work. Yet even though organizations had large work forces, management systems within these organizations were still virtually nonexistent. Organizations had grown in size, but they had not grown in complexity; the systems movement had not yet made its impact upon the organizational setting.

Typically, the work force was organized so that workers were shown a job. If they could not do it, they were fired and quickly replaced. Little, if any, need for supervisor-management training existed. The fastest worker usually became the supervisor, and that worker's job was to set the pace forcing other workers to keep up. Tight discipline, close controls, and constant pressures were the management tools of the day. Attention given to a total performance system was not only considered wasteful, but also an interference with the task of the day—namely, getting the product out the back door.

One of the first people to generate interest in management systems was Frederick W. Taylor. His interest in the field evolved from his observations of laborers. He noted they used the same standardized shovel size to work with no matter what type of material they were carrying. This surprised him because he knew that materials carried in shovels varied considerably in weight. He felt sure that over the years, shovels of different sizes had been devised for carrying different types of materials. Yet evidence disproved this. So he attempted to improve the productivity of laborers by varying shovel size. What he developed as a result was a method of work improvement and greatly increased productivity. With success under his belt, he was prompted to investigate whether his methods might not be applied by supervisors in a variety of work settings.

Several things resulted. First, his experiments gave rise to intensified interest and increasing efficiency of workers. Industrial engineering, for example, is a direct result of Taylor's work. Second, these studies prompted people to begin to look at the practice of management itself and to recognize that a manager's activity is distinct from the activity of subordinate workers. Third, these studies led to further developments in the examination of organizations from a systems point of view.

Taylor's approach was from an engineering and technical point of view. Further changes in management attitudes came with World War II. These changes were not revolutionary but they were important because they were the first steps in the evolution of a systems approach to managing people. The rapid expansion of industry to meet the war needs and the siphoning off of manpower for the armed services, combined with the closing of the European supply source forced many industries to seek new ways of maintaining output.

During the 1950s and 1960s, however, people began to look at organization and management systems from a different point of view: the human point of view of the behavioral scientists invaded mahogany row as organizations began looking for methods of improving worker productivity. The human relations movement was under way. It grew quickly, gaining momentum daily. The most significant aspect of this movement was its focus on managerial interest in people, not things. Before, emphasis had been almost exclusively on things—machines, assembly lines, tools, productions, and other hard technologies. By the mid-1950s, an increased interest in people had become especially noticeable. Managers found they could determine rather accurately how an applicant might do on the job. Psychologists conducted motivational studies. Lectures on what makes people tick were increasingly popular, as were management development programs. Sociologists studied small group behavior; cultural anthropologists observed social variables in corporations (and found some similarities to primitive tribal rites). The age of the behavioral scientists was upon us and the manager put their findings into practice.

As the trend developed and gained momentum, an understanding of systems became essential. One who studies "assemblage of objects" or people united by some form of interaction or interdependence, is such a person. In some cases, this was an operations researcher who applied queuing theory to an inventory control problem. In others, the individual was a public administrator who implemented zero-base budgeting systems in a municipality. The systems person was also a human factor engineer investigating the relationship between workers and machines. One behavioral psychologist utilized a general systems model to analyze human performance problems in organizations. This model is a particularly useful tool for analyzing and solving these problems, and it is with this model that this book is concerned.

A systems model can help us understand human behavior in the organizational context and predict what will happen when a change is made in one of the elements of the model; herein lies its usefulness. If a model is too complicated for practical application or not helpful in analyzing and solving human performance problems, then it is not useful. However, our model is representative of relationships in a system; and we will use it to examine these relationships.

People examine organizations from different points of view. An industrial engineer taking a group tour through a manufacturing plant looks at manufacturing systems, machine timing, line delays, and things that others in the group might not see. An accountant, by contrast, looks for steps and procedures that ensure material was being used as required, job tickets were being turned in, time was being accounted for properly, and that rework costs were charged back to the originating department. The behavioral scientist studies people and work groups, how they interact with one another, and other elements that indicate problems in the human side of the organization. A recent college graduate from an industrial relations program sees things that a veteran worker in the plant does not, and vice versa. On return from the plant tour, in listening to a description of what the others saw, each tour member would no doubt be amazed at how much he or she had missed. If we made a list of what each saw and reported, we would have a fairly complete description of plant operations. The systems approach, in effect, enables us to do this. It is a method of providing us information on the interaction of various elements of the organizational system. In using one systems approach, we can review the organization as a whole or we can examine in detail any particular part of it, such as a department or an operation.

Most systems take something from their environment, change it, and then release the changed product or service into the environment again. For purposes of discussion, let us call what is taken into the system an "input" and what is released from the system an "output." Inputs are raw materials with which the system works and outputs are the products of that system. The raw materials, or inputs, can be changed in many ways. They can be changed in form, as iron ore into steel, or they can be changed in location, as moving potatoes from farm to market. Inputs can also be changed by adding to or subtracting from them, for example, by adding chocolate to milk or by separating wheat from chaff. Whatever form this change takes, let us call the change in the input a "process."

At the simplest level, a system consists of inputs, processes, and outputs (Figure 2.1). An amoeba is a simple system. The amoeba

FIGURE 2.1   The simplest system

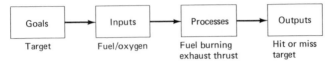

FIGURE 2.2   A system with goals

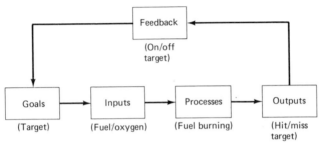

FIGURE 2.3   A guided system with feedback

takes nourishment from the environment, changes that nourishment, and exists on the changed matter.

A somewhat more complex system is one in which we can establish goals before inputs are released, for example, a ballistic system. A rocket is a ballistic system. By present standards, a rocket is a crude mechanism. Armed with a warhead, it moves from its launching pad toward its ultimate target thrusted by powerful engines. Once it leaves its launching pad, however, all human control over flight direction is lost. The rocket is a system (see Figure 2.2), but a crude form of system. It has a goal, inputs, processes, and outputs, but it has no ability to change its direction. It is an unguided missile. It charges ahead unchecked even if it is going in the wrong direction. If our rocket gets off course, we have one of two choices. First, we might blow up the rocket in midair by some remote mechanism, preventing it from landing in a wrong area. Second, we might allow the rocket to proceed ahead and run the risk of the rocket's landing on an inappropriate target. Instead of blowing up the enemy's capital, it might blow up the capital of one of our allies.

Another system form is the guided system (see Figure 2.3). It is a more sophisticated version of a rocket, for it not only has goals, inputs, processes, and outputs, but it also can change direction and alter its course. The key element that distinguishes a guided system from an unguided system is its feedback mechanism, which provides directional control over it even after launching. This feedback mechanism is continually checking actual flight against the flight plan. Once off course, the necessary calculations can be made that put the missile back on course. This is done by comparing the missile's output (its direction) with criteria for what output should be at that point. If the missile is on course, it proceeds as is; if it is off course, alterations are made in amounts of resources used (oxygen, fuel) and the processes (fuel burning). The result is a direction more closely aligned with the goal—which has remained unchanged.

General systems theory suggests that the most useful model for examining organizations from a systems point of view is a living or adaptive system. Living systems must be capable of adapting to their environment as well as influencing their environment. Likewise with organizations; if organizations are not adaptive, then they die out like the brontosaurus, a dinosaur that became extinct because it was unable to adapt to changes in its environment.

A living being has several characteristics. First, it has goals, direction, or purpose. Before the inputs are released into the system and before the processes take place and outputs are released from the system, direction in the form of goals and objectives has been given to the organizational system. Moreover, something that is living can modify its goal based upon feedback from its environment.

Second, a living being can use feedback and can "learn." While organizations do not learn in the formal sense of the word (i.e., in a classroom or a workshop), they can learn from feedback from their environment. For instance, manufacturers find out from consumers through the marketplace (a form of feedback) how they are doing in terms of their product development and marketing techniques. This feedback is the mechanism by which an organization learns.

Third, a living being derives energy from its outside environment and makes use of, or processes, this energy. So, too, with an organization. The inputs into the organization are imported from the outside environment and processed within the organizational context.

Finally, a living being returns something to its environment. What an organization returns to the environment should have more value than the resources that it used up. If an organization does not return more to its environment than it consumes in resources, the organization is bankrupting itself. A market economy organization literally goes bankrupt because it cannot continue to return to its environment goods and services (outputs) with lesser value than the people, materials, and money (inputs) used to produce those goods and services. Customers will buy less and less of its product, probably at a lower and lower price, and the organization eventually ceases to exist.

Organizations, in the public sector, however, such as hospitals, municipalities, state and federal government, and the like, bankrupt themselves not literally but figuratively. Most public-sector organizations operate on a "budget economy" and, with a few notable exceptions, have been able to continue going back to the well to draw on more resources regardless of how they misuse those resources. Thus, the reason some public-sector (and for that matter, some private-sector) organizations have continued to exist in the face of misspent resources is the availability of additional funds from friendly sources.

The word "system" suggests something that is made up of parts that, in turn, are related in an orderly fashion. A living system is a goal-directed entity composed of interrelated parts that have observable goals, inputs, processes, and outputs with a feedback mechanism to provide the organization with learning capability. The learning ability also enables the living system to change its goals.

This type of system is the most useful not only in developing performance objectives for an organization but also in examining human performance problems within the organization. This system can be used in managing all types of employees from the highly creative to those who have marginal or limited skills. This model is also useful in analyzing the aspects or causes of human performance problems and in designing effective practical solutions for the organizational setting.

The five basic components of a living system that give a total performance system methodology for examining human performance in organizations are (1) inputs, (2) processes, (3) outputs, (4) feedback, and (5) goals. This is a homeostatic organization. The term "homeostatic" is typically applied to organisms but it can be applied equally well to organizations. Homeostasis is the condition of being self-regulating. Thermostats, for example, are homeostatic. Goals—here, a desired temperature setting—are plugged into the system, inputs (oxygen and fuel) are taken into the system and processed (in the form of a fire), and outputs (heated air) are released back into the system. There is also a feedback mechanism that regulates the furnace system to achieve the goal—the desired temperature. The furnace receives information from the thermostat. When it registers a temperature below the one that has been established as desired, more inputs are taken into the system, processed, and released as heated air until the desired temperature is reached and the furnace automatically shuts off. Organizations, too, must operate with a homeostatic ap-

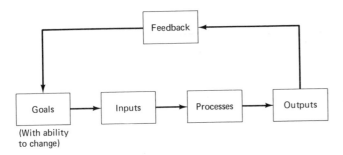

FIGURE 2.4   A living system

proach. Like the thermostat, the organization system is an integrated plan with a feedback mechanism that monitors activity, measures progress, and marks achievement. It tells where we have been, where we are, and where we are going.

The ballistic system we discussed had inputs, processing activities, and outputs. It could go somewhere, but it could not correct course nor change target. Absent, too, was the linking together or integration of the parts of the system so that inputs and processing activities could be regulated—not as effective to the organization as the homeostatic system.

A more useful kind of system in the organizational setting is the guided system. The guided system has a built-in method for evaluating output and feeding back that evaluation so that inputs and outputs are connected. The guided missile and the thermostat are guided systems. Both have a built-in system that regulates performance and corrects course. But they still suffer the disadvantage of not being able to change their goals or seek new targets.

A living system by contrast has the same five components (inputs, processes, outputs, feedback, goals), but with an important added difference. Not only can a living system evaluate its product and feed back the evaluation information so that process activities can be modified as necessary, correcting its performance; but this system also has the ability to change its goal or seek a new target. This model provides the most useful model for examining human performance problems in organizations.

This general model (see Figure 2.5) can be applied to a variety of organizational settings. In a hospital, for instance, the inputs that enter the system are sick people, potentially sick people, aides, medical staff, and so on. Processes that are carried out are surgical operations, medication dispersal, examinations, and physical therapy, to mention a few.

The outputs of the system take the form, for example, of average

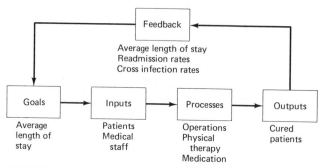

FIGURE 2.5   A hospital as a living system

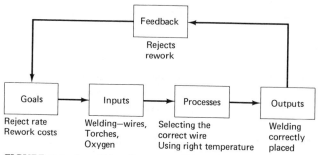

FIGURE 2.6   A welding department as a living system

length of stay and readmission rates. In an adaptive system, goals are established at the beginning. Goals or objectives in this hospital example are what we would expect the average patient length of stay to be, the average linen costs per patient day, and so on. Criteria regarding these goals are planned. Through a variety of feedback mechanisms, information on organization performance—how well the organization is succeeding in meeting its goals—is continually fed back into the system. As long as the organization is on target, it can maintain its present utilization of resources and processes. When feedback shows, however, that the organization may be off target, inputs can be rearranged or processing activity can be changed so that the output can be modified to match more closely the desired target.

An organization that is an adaptive living system can change its target. Feedback mechanisms might say, for instance, that the average length of stay is consistent with what we would hope, but because of a change in medical technology or a meeting with the board of trustees or some other "mechanism," the target is changed and the average length of stay perhaps shortened. Organizations then have to make changes in inputs and processes so that the outputs once again match the new target.

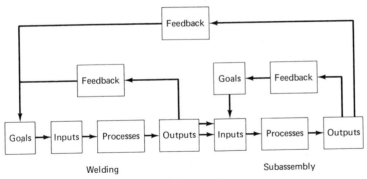

FIGURE 2.7   Linking welding to subassembly

A welding operation provides a different example of how a general systems model works in a different type of organization (see Figure 2.6). This operation has inputs (welding, wire, torches, oxygen), processes (the welding operation), and outputs (weldments correctly placed). It also has targets set at the beginning and feedback that tells how well it is meeting those targets.

Let us use this to show how two or more systems might be linked together effectively (Figure 2.7). We will call the welding department the "processing system" and the subassembly department the "receiving system." The three points of linkage between the two systems are as follows:

1. The outputs of the processing system become the inputs of the receiving system.
2. A feedback loop exists between the receiving system input and the output of the processing system.
3. A receiving system feedback loop exists between the output of the receiving system and the input of the processing system.

When we link together systems like this we can examine the total organization and its performance in light of its operating subsystems. In this situation, for example, the outputs of the welding department become part of the inputs of the subassembly department. Subassembly takes the outputs of the welding department as inputs (combined with other inputs), processes them in certain ways, and produces outputs. Like the hospital and the welding department, they also have goals and a feedback loop to measure the performance of their processes (with outputs) against the desired target or goal.

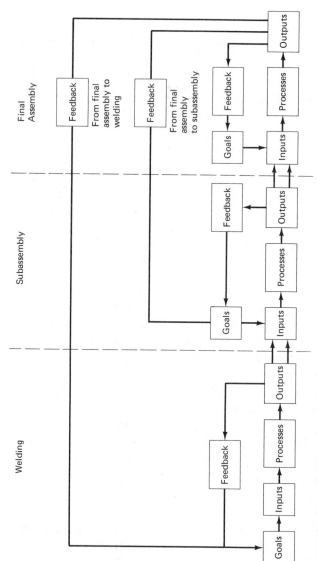

FIGURE 2.8 A total performance system

22

It is also possible to link the subassembly and final assembly departments, making another interrelationship among departments of the organization (Figure 2.8).

There are four ways of examining the assembly operation of this particular firm:

1. We can examine just the welding department.
2. We can examine just the subassembly department.
3. We can examine the final assembly department.
4. We can examine the interrelationship among all three of these departments and regard their interrelationship as a total performance system.

We are concerned in this book with this total performance system. Looking at organizations and departments from a total systems point of view gives the opportunity to examine not only the individual elements of each system, but also the interrelationships of the different subsystems within the organization. The total systems point of view provides as well a methodology for examining the performance of the total organization.

3

Behavior
and
Performance
in
Organizations

HISTORICAL PERSPECTIVE OF BEHAVIORISM
IN BUSINESS AND INDUSTRY

The early applications of behavioral technology in business and industry began in the early 1960s. The pioneering applications occurred at the University of Michigan at what was then called the Bureau of Industrial Relations and has since been renamed the Division of Management Education. Previously, behavioral technology had been applied in both the school setting and the clinical setting but not in the business setting. The transition from the school and clinical environments to the business environment had not yet been made on any meaningful scale.

An early transition into the business environment occurred through the use of programmed instruction in a form of self-paced and individualized construction. Participants in programmed learning workshops studied how to write programmed materials for use in their own organizations. Many of the early developers of programmed instruction techniques were behavioral psychologists. Programmed learning began to generate an interest in the industrial applications of behavioral technology. Designers of instructional materials for business and industry very closely followed the applications in the development of self-instructional texts in the school setting. It was with this somewhat inauspicious beginning that behavioral technology made its first entrance into the business world.

The real transition came, however, when trainers discovered that many well-designed training programs failed when applied on the job because the job situation did not support the new skills that had been developed through carefully planned training efforts. In many cases, this was caused by a discrepancy between the behavior called for by the training program and the behavior that was supported in the job environment.

In analyzing the failure of well-conceived and well-designed training programs, we note that a common pattern begins to develop. An employee enters the training situation with a certain repertoire of job skills. Let's call this repertoire the "pretraining skill level." During the course of training, certain other skills are developed and the employee reenters the job situation with a new skill level that we call the "post-training skill level."

For a short period of time, the employee performs at this new, higher level of skill. Within a relatively short time, however, the employee begins to regress. Newly acquired skills fall by the wayside and lie dormant. Within a relatively short time, the employee has regressed from the post-training skill level to the pretraining skill level.

One retail establishment found this out the difficult way. Over a period of about a year, they put together a very well-designed, carefully-thought-out, multimedia training package intended to teach the sales clerks all the selling skills necessary to do a good job. Among other things, sales clerks were taught how to fill out forms correctly, how to make sure that merchandise was arranged in the most eye-appealing way, how to determine customer needs, how to select clothing for customers designed to meet both articulated and unarticulated needs, how to help customers choose between one piece of merchandise and another, how to overcome objections, how to sell related merchandise, and how to close a sale.

Bursting with energy and confidence generated by their newly developed skills, sales clerks graduated from the course and were placed on the selling floor, where their newly acquired skills began to fall by the wayside. First, they discovered that filling out the forms was not as easy on the job as it was in class. Forms were poorly designed, and it was much easier and less time consuming to fill them out improperly. The pure selling skills of identifying needs, asking for the order, and selling related merchandise seemed much easier to do in the classroom than on the job. These skills were especially more difficult to put in practice on the job because there was little if any feedback or support from customers on employee effectiveness.

In the classroom, the instructor was there to help. Not so on the floor. Moreover, because of the role play situation in the classroom, a one-to-one success ratio was experienced. In other words, just about everytime a student tried something, it worked in one way or another. However, on the job, sales clerks encountered a different breed of cat—the real customer. The success ratio in selling related merchandise, for example, fell to about one-to-nine; thus, each employee had one success experience for every ten tries, giving a ratio of one success to nine failures. While a ratio of one to nine is one that an experienced sales clerk might be able to tolerate and to work with, a newly trained sales clerk generally cannot live with such a record. In addition to their ratio of only one success to nine failures, some of those failures were extremely punishing. Customers became upset, even visibly angry when the sales clerk tried to sell them related merchandise. The same held true for approaching a customer on the floor. When observing a customer entering the department for the first time, the sales clerks were supposed to go over unobtrusively to the customer and say something such as, "That's a nice jacket you're looking at; it is part of our new spring line and is both wrinkle free and water resistant." The newly trained sales clerks followed this approach with vigor the first week on the job. However, they found out that it did not pay in all situations, and they soon began to take a more passive attitude toward helping customers when they first entered the department. The newly trained sales clerks thus found some negative aspects to performing in the desired manner. More importantly, they found no support or reinforcement for behaving as suggested by the training department. The department head never gave the clerks any feedback on how they were making the transition from the training class to the actual job situation. In fact, very little was ever said to them except when they made a particularly blatant or obvious error.

Within a few short weeks, the clerks were back at their pretraining skill level and sales began to taper off again. Line management lambasted the training department for designing "another expensive training package that didn't work." The fact is that there was nothing wrong with the training package, but that both line management and the training department had failed to take into account other factors present in the job situation.

In another instance of analyzing the causes of training failure, a telephone company found it was losing a considerable amount of money because its installers were not noting when they had to install a phone in facilities with a dropped ceiling. In those instances, the installers had to use more wire than in normal installations. This process is called a ceiling drop, which imposes an additional charge for the installation. The phone company spent a great deal of money teaching the installers how to recognize the situation that called for a ceiling drop, how to explain it to the customer, and how to fill it out properly on the form. All the installers participated in an intensive training program designed to teach them skills necessary to handle the situation. The company figured its annual loss due to the installation of uncharged ceiling drops was close to a quarter of a million dollars. Within the first week after the training, the company could already tell the difference. More ceiling drops were being turned in, and it was anticipated that the difference in revenue would be close to the quarter of a million dollars a year. However, after a few more weeks the number of ceiling drops reported by the installers had diminished considerably and the company was once again losing money on services it performed but were not paid for by the customer.

A specialist in training design was called in to find out why the training had failed. She noted a curious thing. The form that the installers were required to fill out was extremely complicated and the part dealing with ceiling drops was even more complicated. She suggested that the problem was not due to a lack of knowledge on the part of the installers but was rather due to a performance deficiency on the job. The job situation (in this case, the job form) was making it too difficult to perform using the newly acquired skills.

The specialist therefore recommended a change in the form to make it simpler to complete. One small change was made by adding a box where the installer could merely check "ceiling drop installed." Now the installer no longer had to fill out an extensive explanation of what took place in the house. Within one week after the change in the form, the number of ceiling drops reported and charged back to the customers had increased dramatically, far above what it was immediately after the training sessions. Thus, by redesigning the job situation so that it more fully supported the training that had taken place, the company was able to realize the full potential of its training program.

The failure of well-designed training programs to change employee behavior substantially on the job for any extended period of time has been termed by Geary Rummler of Praxis Corporation as the "can do, will do" concept. After the training, employees *can* perform correctly but *do not* simply because the job environment does not support their newly acquired skills. Staff members of the University of Michigan began to concern themselves with this phenomenon. They began examining the application of behavioral technology to ensure that newly acquired skills were supported on the job.

This change in emphasis led to a shift from merely the development of self-instruction materials to an analysis of why performance does or does not occur in the job situation. Those involved in the analysis found an interesting thing: many training problems could be solved by nontraining solutions merely by a simple change in the job situation. So emphasis in the application of behavioral technology moved from the design of training programs to the analysis of why training programs did not take place and why skills developed in the programs were not used in the job situation to the full application of behavioral technology to change employee performance on the job.

Concerned with this phenomenon, Dr. Karen Brethower, a fellow staff member at the University of Michigan during the 1960s and a pioneer in the application of behavioral technology in business and industry, has suggested that the use of behavioral technology in organizations is particularly relevant in these three primary ways:

1. In defining the specific response or behavior you want.
2. In building an environment conducive to that response.
3. In providing consequences congruent with what we stated we want.

With these points in mind, staff members at Michigan began to build a technology of changing employee behavior that has proven itself in bottom line payoffs in all types of organizations.

BEHAVIOR, PERFORMANCE, AND MANAGEMENT

What is Behavior?

Behavior is an activity that can be seen, measured, or described. Writing this book was a behavior on my part. Reading the book is a behavior on your part. If after reading it you return to your job situation and apply some of the principles, techniques, and concepts described in the book, your job behavior will change; that is, you will do certain things differently after reading the book. If the book has its intended effect, those job behaviors that are different in the future will improve the performance of people who report to you, as well as those who work around you.

One of the problems in examining employee behavior is that the term "behavior" generally connotes that a certain behavior is "bad." It is difficult to tell exactly why this has happened because the behaviorist does not use the connotation except as job behaviors affect employee performance. Here are a list of behaviors that would presumably be "good" on a job: filling out a sales slip correctly, making calls, thanking a customer, using the customer's name in answering the phone, smiling, submitting reports on time, placing parts in the right bin, and coming to work on time. Each of these behaviors is "good" in the sense that it presumably leads to some desired result and improves the overall job performances of the employee. Moreover, carried one step further, these behaviors should contribute significantly to overall organizational results.

On the other hand, here are some behaviors that are "bad": spilling ashes on the floor, shouting at a customer, not submitting expense reports, coming to work late or not at all, producing excessive numbers of poor parts, and filling out a sales slip improperly. Each of these behaviors detracts from employee performance and reduces overall organizational performance.

Behavior becomes "good" or "bad" only when we can attach some value to it. The behaviorist attaches this value in looking at end organizational results and examining which behaviors will accomplish these end results.

The question "What can we do to change an employee behavior?" often brings an adverse reaction from managers. Yet the question must be asked, for only when we ask it then answer it can we significantly contribute to positive organizational results. Although the idea of managing behavior change is an anathema to many managers, they engage in this technique every day whether they are aware of it or not. They engage in the techniques of managing behavior change not only with their staff members, but also with many, if not most, individuals with whom they come in contact every day. The thought of modifying behavior deliberately and systematically appears to many to smack of manipulation and control, or it seems to be degrading to the individual whose behavior is being changed. Changing employee behavior encounters both intellectual and emotional resistance, yet in the practice of management, a great many widely accepted management techniques simply are methodologies designed to change employee behavior.

Take the word "delegation." Delegation is considered to be a sound management practice. An effective manager must be an effective delegator. Some of the principles of effective delegation include (1) determining the tasks to be delegated and who will do them, (2) ensuring that the employee has the tools to do tasks properly, (3) explaining the importance of delegated tasks to the employee, (4) following up to make sure things are going smoothly, (5) making sure the employee has learned from the principle and has applied it equally well in other situations.

If we talk to a manager who has delegated some tasks to one of his subordinate staff members and inquire as to his management practices, he would perhaps suggest that he is a pretty good delegator. If, however, we ask that same manager, "Would you be interested in some techniques for changing employee behavior?", we might see him put up a red flag. He might even question the morality of purposefully deciding to change employee behavior, ask whether or not it was proper for a manager to use these techniques, and perhaps even suggest that attempts to change employee behavior smack not only of big brotherism but of paternalism and manipulative control besides. Yet, that is exactly what the manager is trying to do when he seeks to delegate more tasks to his staff members.

Management is often described as the business of getting things done through other people. Some describe it as making things happen. No matter how we look at it, management is getting other people to do the things that have to be done. It is clearly a practice that implies we are going to have to manage other people's behavior. The effective manager is one who is able to manage other individuals' behaviors, ensuring that the behavior changes take place.

In today's changing economic and sociopolitical environment, a variety of people must perform the task of managing other individuals' behavior. Let's take a look at a sales manager, for instance (Figure 3.1). This sales manager has five sales representatives (rep.) reporting to him. If we ask him what kind of tasks he undertakes in

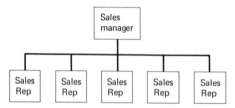

FIGURE 3.1   Traditional view of sales managers' management function

relationship to his sales force, it will be clear that he manages their behaviors. He tries, for instance, to get them to close a higher percentage of calls, to make more calls, to increase sales of high-margin items, to increase the penetration of new products, and to submit their calls and expense reports on time.

If we look at the sales manager from another point of view (see Figure 3.2), we see that he must interact with other departments and other organizations. He must interact with engineering departments, manufacturing departments, credit and collection departments, and advertising agencies. In these interactions, he manages the behavior of others. Although he does not manage them in the traditional sense of the word (that is, having them report to him on a direct organizational basis), he nevertheless "manages" them by enlisting their aid in projects, getting them to commit themselves to certain things, and making sure they follow through on these commitments. Importantly, he manages them by persuading them to engage in behaviors that are supportive of his sales efforts and to desist from behaviors that are counterproductive to his sales efforts.

Managing the behaviors of people in other departments and organizations is often a more complex task than managing behavior change among one's own staff. This manager has more sanctions to impose on those employees who report directly to him than on individuals who do not report directly to him. More and more in today's rapidly changing organizational world, it is the individual who is effective in both types of situations (managing individuals who report directly to him as well as those who do not) that is the best leader or manager.

The effective manager is someone who is able to change positively the behavior of those who come in contact with him or her so

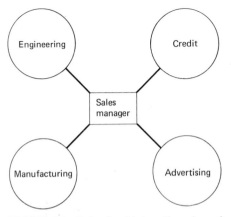

FIGURE 3.2   Behavioral interaction view of sales managers' function

that they are supportive of both the task that must be accomplished and his or her objectives. Good leaders and motivators are individuals who through a variety of techniques are able to get their staff to engage in those behaviors they consider necessary to achieve their goals. Managers who deliberately set out to change employee behavior and admit this are much farther ahead of their colleagues who motivate employees to "change their attitudes" or "affect their personalities." A behavioral technologist or behavioral psychologist does deliberately and with foresight what many managers do in a haphazard, random fashion. Managers who use behavioral technology to get their staff to do the job are merely doing with foresight and in a carefully planned fashion what they formerly did haphazardly—changing employee behavior. If we examine other methods people use to influence employee behavior, we see they are actually trying to change that behavior, even though they may not call it that.

Personality and Behavior

"Harry has a lousy personality," we hear a manager complain. "What we need to do is get Harry to change his personality." "What," we might ask, "needs to be changed in Harry's personality?" "Well," the reply comes back, "Harry is too aggressive and what we have to do is make him not so aggressive." The nonbehaviorist manager in this situation then sets about trying to change Harry's personality so that he is less aggressive. He does it haphazardly, not knowing exactly what "aggressiveness" is, but knowing he doesn't like Harry to show this trait. He counsels Harry and tells him to be less aggressive on his sales calls so that he does not antagonize customers. Harry, reacting to his nonbehavior-oriented manager and being unsure of what "aggressive" means, overreacts and not only is less aggressive, but finally gets to the point where he must force himself to muster up courage to knock on somebody's door when making his next call.

The behaviorist approaches the situation with a different point of view. If a manager were to say to the behavioral technologist, "We have to do something about Harry—he's too aggressive," the behaviorist first asks, "What does Harry do that leads you to conclude he is aggressive?" "Well," the answer comes back, "I guess there are three things: first, he puts his feet on customers' desk while he is talking; second, he barges into customers' offices without being invited; and third, Harry loves to smoke cigars. While cigar smoking is okay, it would be much better if he would not light up a victory cigar until after he has left the customers' office and if he would refrain from reaching across customers' desks to get the ashtray for his matches and ashes." "Aha," says the behaviorist, "There is something I can deal with. There are several specifics in Harry's behavior that we have to change. First, we have to change the behavior of his putting his feet on the desk; second, we have to change the behavior of his not waiting to be invited into the office; and third, we have to change some of his cigar smoking behavior. Not all of it, but some of it."

We can see approaches in the two examples that on the surface might appear close to each other; in fact, they are strikingly different. The nonbehaviorist deals with general abstractions ("I don't like his aggressiveness"). The behaviorist deals with specific behaviors (cigar smoking, feet on the desk, etc.) that need to be changed to improve Harry's job effectiveness. One reason the behavioral approach is more effective than the traditional is that it deals with specifics. To the behaviorist personality is nothing more than a collection of behaviors. If we were to change Harry's three offensive sets of behaviors so that they were not counterproductive to his sales effort, the sales manager might conclude that Harry had undergone a dramatic personality change. In fact, Harry's basic personality is probably unchanged, but he has shown substantial behavior changes.

Motivation and Behavior

The same case can be made for the relationship between motivation and behavior. Talk to enough managers about their staff performance and sooner or later you will run into a manager who says, "What I really need are some techniques to motivate my staff. They are not motivated enough."

This individual means that for some reason or other his or her staff is not performing adequately. If the individuals were motivated, they would perform up to the level of responsibility required by the job. If somebody's behavior pattern conforms to our model expectations of that job, we tend to say he or she is motivated; if the behavior pattern does not conform to our job expectations, we have a tendency to say that individual is poorly motivated. Behaviorists deal with this situation in much the same manner as they would deal with the person who is seeking help with Harry's personality. For instance, take the manager who says, "I have a problem with my press operators, they are not motivated. I don't know exactly just what it is, but they just don't seem to want to work hard anymore. You know, people aren't motivated the way they used to be when I was young." "I can sympathize with that," says the behaviorist, probing further. "What kinds of things do they do on the job and what kinds of things don't they do on the job that leads you to conclude they are not motivated." "Well, take, for example, Mary," says the manager. "Mary comes in late about three times a week and she is absent at least five days a month." "Aha," the behaviorist would say, "There is something with which we can deal. Rather than trying to motivate Mary, let's see what we can do about changing her job behavior. Specifically, we have two job behaviors to change. First, we have to

TABLE 3.1   Nonbehaviors, Behaviors, and Results

Nonbehaviors	Behaviors	Results of Behavior
Bad attitude	Filling out a sales slip	Production volume
Motivated	correctly	Quality level
Friendly	Making cold calls	Cost of rework
Courteous	Thanking a customer	Scrap rates
Aggressive	Giving the customer's name	Direct costs
Neat	Answering the phone	Indirect costs
Angry	Smiling	Safety
Cheerful	Wearing a tie	Housekeeping
Irritating	Shouting at a customer	Suggestions
Pleasant	Saying "good morning"	Grievances
	Spilling ashes on the floor	Schedules
	Submitting reports on time	Sales volume
	Placing parts in the right	Cost of sales
	bin	Gross margin
	Coming to work on time	Mark ups
		Mark downs
		Reports
		Crew size
		Operating cost per unit
		Service requests
		Salary cost per unit
		Overhead per unit
		Receiving and shipping cost per unit
		Turnover
		Complaints
		Cost savings
		Quotas
		Tardiness
		Absenteeism
		Turnaround time
		Number of vendor contacts
		Average order size

change the behavior of not coming to work on time and second, we have to change the behavior of not coming to work at all."

Behaviorists put themselves in a somewhat different position than most people when examining that job performance. They look for specific examples of behavior that contribute to organizational results or absence of results and then determine the relationship between job behavior and job performance. They are not concerned with changing a behavior that does not affect job performance. Behaviorists make a very important distinction between general abstractions ("they aren't motivated") and job behavior ("she comes in late three times a week"). They don't deal with abstractions but with specific behavior patterns. Moreover, behaviorists look for a relationship between a behavior that needs to be changed and improvement of organizational performance. An experimental psychologist may change behaviors such as the use of certain words, classroom activities of children, or students' actions in research projects to test theories or hypotheses about what affects human behavior. In contrast, behavioral psychologists working in an organization look at job-related behavior and try to increase the number and amount of behaviors that are helping move organizational performance in the right direction. They seek techniques of reducing or altogether eliminating those behaviors that are counterproductive to job performance. Table 3.1 illustrates the different relationships between general abstractions of nonbehaviors, specific behaviors, and the organizational results that are affected by those behaviors. Nonbehaviorists deal primarily with items in Column 1. They make statements such as, "We need to improve attitude around here." Behaviorists, on the other hand, deal primarily with the second and third columns. They ask, "Profits need to be improved. What employee behaviors we are not now getting do we need to improve profits? What behaviors that we now get do we want to eliminate because they are counterproductive to profits?"

SEEKING HIGH-IMPACT AREAS FOR IMPROVEMENT

Most managers are well acquainted with Pareto's Law, formulated by Vilfredo Pareto. Pareto was an economist who observed that results and causes of results were not equally distributed. His findings are also known as the 20–80 principle, which suggests that

- 20 percent of inventory items account for 80 percent of inventory dollars.

- 20 percent of all employees account for 80 percent of scrap.
- 20 percent of customers are responsible for 80 percent of complaints.
- 20 percent of the product line accounts for 80 percent of gross margin dollars.

The ratio is not always 20–80, of course. It might be that 15 percent of inventory items account for 82 percent of inventory dollars, or 26 percent of all employees account for 91 percent of scrap. The 20–80 ratio is not always exact but its principle is valid. The principle is merely this: some vital few of something account for the majority of the results that are obtained.

Applying the 20–80 principle to employee behavior suggests that 20 percent of the job behaviors in which an employee engages account for 80 percent of the results that the employee contributes to the organization (see Figure 3.3).

The manager's task is, of course, identifying behaviors that play the important role and behaviors that are counterproductive, then changing employee behavior accordingly.

Let's take as an example a company with inventory shrinkage caused by shortages in vendor shipments. Let's peg that at $1 million a year. Further, assume that because of shipping schedules and a variety of other factors, most shipments come in within a six- or seven-day period at the beginning of the month. Here are some of the behaviors in which an employee might engage who is concentrating on checking these incoming shipments:

1. Checking all shipments.
2. Checking shipments of certain vendors.
3. Checking shipments of certain items.
4. Checking a specified number of shipments each day.
5. Checking a random stratified sample of shipments over the period of one month.

We can see from this list that a number of potential employee behaviors will move us toward our objective of reducing inventory shrinkage due to shortages in vendor shipments. However, suppose the employees do not have time to engage in all the behaviors. Then some behaviors must be selected over others. An important part of behavioral technology is selecting behaviors with higher payoff than others. The 20–80 principle helps us identify those behaviors. It tells

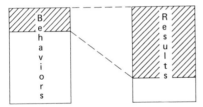

FIGURE 3.3   How behavior change can affect results

us, for example, that 20 percent of vendors account for 80 percent of shortages. One behavior in which we want the employee to engage, then, is checking the shipments of vendors known to be continually shorting us, whether deliberately or by error.

It is probably a fair assumption that not all purchased parts are of equal value. There is a considerable difference in value between 100 transmissions, 100 batteries, and 100 light bulbs. We can, then, sort our vended parts into A, B, and C priority items depending upon usage patterns and values. We might want checkers of incoming shipments to check all shipments of A parts, 50 percent of the shipments of B parts, and maybe only 25 percent of the shipments of C parts. Thus, the high-priority behaviors that contribute most significantly to results are checking shipments of vendors who have a recognized pattern of short shipments, then checking the A, B, and C priority items as described.

The task of the behavioral technologist is twofold: first, to identify high-impact behaviors that contribute significantly to organizational results and then to take steps to ensure that those behaviors occur on the job; second, to identify behaviors that are counterproductive to results and take steps to see they do not occur as often or not at all.

Start such an analysis with the result or the job accomplishments. Only if there is a deficiency there does it make sense to back up a step and look at the behaviors that need changing. Sometimes very small changes in behavior produce a very significant change in job performance. Let's consider, for example, two salesmen, Mr. Smart and Mr. Dumb. If we look at the results of their job performance, we find four areas in which they are expected to accomplish results:

1. Number of new accounts per month.

2. Dollar volume generated per year.

3. Average order size.

4. Percentage of market penetration in their territory.

When we look at the results:

	Smart	Dumb
Average Number of New Accounts per Month	17	3
Yearly $ Volume	$847,000	$236,000
Average Order Size	1,200	800
Market Penetration	6%	1.2%

we see that Mr. Smart clearly outperforms Mr. Dumb. In fact, if we look only at the results, we might well conclude that Mr. Dumb was so incompetent that it wouldn't be worth trying to get him to perform up to standard.

However, when we examine the sales call behavior of both Mr. Smart and Mr. Dumb, we find that both of them perform very nearly correctly. It is only in one small area that we find the behavior deficiency in Mr. Dumb: he fails to ask for the order. Everything else required of him in making a sales call he does well. If we could change but one small behavior, we could make a substantial impact on his total job performance, including such areas as number of new accounts per month, dollar volume generated per year, average order size, and average market penetration in his territory.

This situation is analogous to an electrical utility heating water to 211 degrees Fahrenheit. If the utility has heated its water to only 211 degrees, this hot water will not generate electricity. Add but one degree to that water, however, so that it reaches 212 degrees, and the water begins to boil and produce steam. Steam generates electrical energy that the utility can sell. The difference in water temperature is only one degree, but the difference in terms of accomplishment is quite significant. In changing employee behavior, we are looking for that one-degree change in behavior that will produce substantial results in terms of significant job accomplishments. The reverse is also true, of course. Just as a small change in behavior can produce large improvements in results, a very small deficiency in employee behavior can produce large deficiencies in results.

There are two types of costs to consider in looking at behavior change programs among employees: initial cost and ongoing costs. To maximize the return on our behavior change programs, we should take both of these costs into account. A useful basic formula to determine the priority of behavior-change projects (i.e., where should we start in quality control, manufacturing, marketing, accounting) is

$$V = \frac{AR - OC}{IC} \quad \left(\text{value} = \frac{\text{annual return} - \text{ongoing cost}}{\text{initial cost}} \right)$$

In this formula, V stands for value. It determines this project's priority and the expected return on investment. If that number is less than one, the project is not worth undertaking. It has also been our experience that it is not worthwhile to consider projects with a payoff of only two- or three-to-one. In the formula, AR stands for annual return from the project, that is, the savings expected to be realized annually. OC stands for ongoing costs associated with the behavior change program such as increased computer charges for additional reports, increased number of purchasing clerks for putting additional information on purchase orders, an additional staff member in the accounting department to ensure that the information is sent back to the proper individual, and so on. IC is initial costs, associated with analyzing performance problems, designing solutions, and providing necessary training. Thus, the value of the project is determined by taking the projected annual return or savings from the project, subtracting from that the ongoing costs, and dividing that number by the initial costs. Suppose that we had a project with a projected annual savings of $105,000; ongoing costs associated with the project of $5,000; and analysis, design, training, and implementation costs of $20,000. This gives us a value of five, which means that on an ongoing basis, we will have $5 return for every dollar we invest in the project:

$$V = \frac{105,000 - 5,000}{20,000} = 5$$

This chapter suggests that as managers we look for ways of maximizing employee performance. Clearly, there are direct correlations between employees' behavior on the job and the performance level of each employee. Moreover, there are, or should be, direct correlations between the performance level of the employee and the overall performance of the organization. The behaviorist works backward through the cycle, looking first at organizational performance, then at individual job accomplishments (the performance level), and finally at specific employee behaviors. Not only does examining employee behavior make sense from the viewpoint of behavior, it makes sense from the viewpoint of the manager who must make practical decisions every day. The job of a manager is in fact one of managing the behavior of employees so that desired results of the organization are accomplished. An effective manager is able to elicit effectively from his employees behaviors that are supportive of organizational results; he is likewise able to eliminate employee behaviors that are counterproductive to the organization's success.

Examining employee performance problems from the behaviorist point of view gives the manager a new tool with which to work. Rather than dealing with abstractions such as motivated bad attitude or lousy personality, the manager can now pinpoint specific behaviors that need to be changed and then develop programs for changing them. Small changes in employee behavior can produce dramatic results in job accomplishments. The key to using this tool well is the manner in which performance problems are analyzed. No longer can managers afford to analyze employee performance problems in terms of abstractions. They must now identify specific employee behaviors that need to be changed. Not only do such techniques for identifying and analyzing employee performance problems exist; they have proven themselves to be of great value in developing behavior-change programs with substantial impact upon organizational results.

4

Analyzing Human Performance Problems

The majority of any organization's problems are human performance problems. Yet more attention and resources have been directed toward solving machine-oriented problems. We have been far more successful in solving these machine problems than our people-oriented problems. Amazingly, we have devised sophisticated, nearly miraculous dialysis machines that will function as human kidneys and cleanse blood, but we haven't yet developed a technology that will get the technician to come in on time to operate the machine. We have computerized scheduling systems so that we can be sure the plant is loaded correctly and that materials flow smoothly through the plant, but we can't assure yet that the workers will operate the machinery in such a manner as to reduce scrap. We have systems of time and territory management that allow us to concentrate sales efforts on areas with the highest potential payoff, but we

41

have not been able to get the sales staff to fill out their call reports accurately so that we can keep them moving in the right direction. In short, these solutions that we have developed for organizational problems have focused on hardware. We have avoided tackling problems that focus on human behavior.

One reason for such success in solving machine problems and failing to find solutions to human problems has been the lack of analytic tools for examining human behavior. If a machine breaks down, we can go down a checklist examining whether sprockets, spindle, gears, drive belt, or casting needs repair. But, until recently, we had not devised a checklist for analyzing human performance problems.

Lacking effective tools for analyzing human behavior, we have tried to solve some organizational behavior problems before we have been able to analyze them completely. Incorrect analysis of the problems, unfortunately, has not prevented us from attempting to design solutions to the problems, many times the wrong problems. What results is the common but embarrassing situation of devising complex solutions to the wrong problem. The practicing manager is overwhelmed with solutions to human problems. Sensitivity training, team building, job enrichment, job enlargement, matrix management, and countless other "solutions" to human performance problems abound. The difficulty is that whereas the manager has plenty of material regarding problem solutions, he has almost a complete lack of information on how to analyze human performance problems. We must increase our effectiveness in analyzing people problems if we are to reduce the number and frequency of these problems.

Until recently, the major method for tackling human performance problems has been the internal approach; that is, looking inside the individual to determine his or her needs and interests. Based upon that examination, we categorize the employees and then begin designing a solution looking at their needs and interests. Abraham A. Maslow, as an example of this approach, has identified a hierarchy of needs that helps us in this categorizing.[1] Maslow suggests there are five primary needs with an ascending order of priority (see Figure 4.1).

MASLOW'S HIERARCHY OF NEEDS

Physiological Needs

Physiological needs are the most important in the ranking. They are the basic human needs of rest, food, water, and shelter. Although

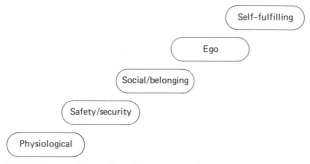

FIGURE 4.1 Hierarchy of human needs

these are the lowest level of needs, they become of paramount importance when unfulfilled. Popular statements to the contrary, we do indeed live by bread alone, if there is no other food available. Except in the most unusual circumstances, security needs, social needs, ego needs, and self-fulfillment needs are meaningless for the hungry. We concentrate our need-fulfillment energies on one or two needs at a time. We devote little energy to more than that either because our other needs have been satisfied or because they are too distant to be of immediate importance. The need for food, for example, has no appreciable effect on individual behavior until one is deprived of it. Deprived of it, fulfilling that basic physiological need to eat becomes of paramount importance.

Need for Security

Fulfilled need ceases to be a motivator, so, when the basic physiological needs are satisfied, the need for safety takes its turn in affecting individual behavior. Once people have food, water, shelter, and other items that provide for basic physical maintenance, the need to be safe and secure must be fulfilled. We turn to establishing order, control, and direction. Factors like job security and predictability of income are important. We want to live in a secure neighborhood and reside in a country relatively free from attack.

The emergence of this need for safety and security can be seen whenever the armed forces announces plans to place a strategic or tactical system within a particular geographic region. Up to that time, individuals living in the region have probably had their need for security fulfilled. The advent of the installation of a new weapon system and tracking station in their backyards threatens their feeling of safety and security. Realizing that the system might be a prime target in time of war, they hold meetings, call and write their congressmen, enlist the help of newspapers and radio stations. Until the citizens' needs for security are met, fulfilling those needs plays a predominant role in determining their behavior.

We can also imagine that if those same individuals were to be placed in a situation where they were deprived of food, water, clothing, and shelter, their energies would be directed toward meeting these needs instead of fulfilling the need for security.

Social Needs

The third category is social needs. They include the desire for belonging, for attention, or for acceptance by peer groups. Manifestations of this particular need find themselves in country club membership, joining a bowling team, or getting involved in some other activity that brings social acceptance to the individual. Fulfilling the social needs becomes important in determining behavior only when the lower needs have been adequately satisfied. Only unsatisfied needs are motivators. Until the physiological and security needs have been met, social and higher-order needs do not greatly affect individual behavior.

Need for Esteem

Our next higher order of needs is for esteem. These relate to the individual's desire for self-respect, self-esteem, self-confidence, achievement, and knowledge. These needs are exceedingly difficult to satisfy. Just as hunger can be felt and satisfied, social needs can be fairly readily identified and almost as readily satisfied. However, unlike the lower-level needs, ego needs are more complex, more difficult to fulfill, and harder to measure. Moreover, different individuals have differing degrees of ego needs.

Since the mid-1960s, we have seen concern for fulfilling this need predominate on the American social scene. Sociologists observe that questions such as "Who am I?" "Where do I fit?" and "What do I think of myself?" are asked with increasing frequency. Courses, books, workshop sessions, and long walks in the woods all have individuals searching for their role in life. New problems begin to arise as human behavior begins to direct itself toward the fulfillment of the ego needs. The criteria by which we judge whether our physiological needs or our security needs or our social needs have been fulfilled are much more clear and far easier to measure than the criteria by which we judge the fulfillment of our need for esteem.

J. B. Ritchie,[2] an astute observer of organizational behavior, notes that identifying and fulfilling ego needs has produced an increasing amount of conflict within our society. Social needs have traditionally been fulfilled by family, work, and social clubs, which were developed, at least historically, to fulfill either social or lower needs. As individuals fulfill these lower-order needs and seek fulfillment of their ego needs, conflict arises. For instance, social conventions may conflict with or hamper the meeting of our ego needs. Ritchie suggests that the conflict between observing social conventions and demanding recognition of one's identity is one of the most significant adjustment problems today's society faces.

Self-Actualization

Self-actualization needs, the final ones in the hierarchy, focus upon the realization of one's own potential. They deal with our desire for self-development and self-fulfillment and our quest for creativity.

Self-actualization is best represented by the expression of "doing your own thing," particularly as used by young people today. Their energies are concentrated upon realizing their own potential and maximizing their psychic return on investment. This highest order of need can be seen in those individuals who act for their own intrinsic satisfaction rather than those who perform an act only because it meets one of the four more basic needs.

FULFILLMENT OF NEEDS

Once we have the necessary amount of food to live, the intensity of effort in acquiring the food begins to diminish, and our need for security emerges. Once these needs have been satisfied, their importance diminishes and higher-order needs emerge. The amount of effort we exert in fulfilling a need corresponds directly to the degree with which that need has been met. This point can be most clearly seen in Figure 4.2.

Each level of need comes strongly into play only as the preceding lower-level needs have been adequately, but not completely, satisfied. The implications of this are far-reaching for the practice of management in organizations. Physiological needs met by the job are fulfilled in the form of wages and salaries that give employees the opportunity to purchase goods and services in the marketplace. Security needs are met by providing protection from physical injury on the job and in offering jobs that are relatively secure. Individuals who are not secure in their job will seek to have this need fulfilled before they seek fulfillment of other needs. Management actions that

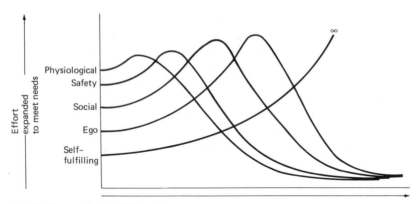

FIGURE 4.2   Need fulfillment

threaten job security through capricious or arbitrary decisions elevate the priority for fulfillment of this need to a very high position within the employee's need scale. This holds for the president of an organization just as it does for the production worker.

Social needs are fulfilled on the job through membership in a work group and through positions in that group. Interestingly, many studies have demonstrated that a tightly knit work team often outperforms a collection of individuals who do not regard themselves as a team. Yet management discourages these teams, assuming that tightly knit teams represent a threat to the organization. By trying to break up, rather than encourage, teams and work groups, management thwarts individuals who are seeking to fulfill their particular social need. When the need is thwarted, members of work groups often become defensive and resistant to change and seek ways to combat management's influence upon the work group.

Ego needs are met on the job by recognition given for work well done; by opportunities for accomplishment, achievement, and independence of action. Self-actualization is met on the job by giving an individual the opportunity to realize his or her full potential. People at this level of need gratification are generally engaged in a continual program of self-development and find that the job itself provides its own intrinsic rewards.

There are several problems with approaches such as this. First, such an approach tends to separate human performance problems from the complex job environment in which these problems occur. Therefore, we begin to presume that the causes of and solutions to the problems are within the individual and are not affected by the job environment. We send an employee off to a course in human relations, communication, or motivation to make him or her "more aware of human needs." Afterward, however, the problems persist.

Second, when we deal with human performance problems, we have built-in biases and assumptions about human nature. It is difficult to view these problems as objectively as we would a machine because our biases get in the way. For instance, some people ascribe certain traits to blacks; many live with stereotypes of women; biases persist about Chicanos for many people. Old people are often considered different from young people; supervisors are different from blue-collar workers, some managers believe; others feel Indians are motivated by different factors than Japanese. Although there are certainly individual differences between employees, our biases about the source of these differences often get in the way of correctly analyzing human performance problems.

Third, the internal approach does not give us a *technology* for analyzing and solving human performance problems. Theories such as this can be useful to corporate staffs in designing policies and procedures that are sensitive to people seeking to fulfill higher hierarchy needs (e.g., self-fulfillment), but they are not of much practical use to the manager trying to solve an immediate performance problem in the plant or to the sales manager with a problem child on his sales force. That manager desperately needs a scientific technology for dealing with human performance problems. The characteristics of such a technology include the following:

1. *Predictability*. We can say in advance what will occur if certain conditions are present in the job situation.
2. *Measurability*. We can not only predict what will happen but we can also measure changes in operational results or changes in employee behavior as the result of instituting changes in the job.
3. *Understandability*. We know the cause-and-effect relationships between the behavioral events we are examining.
4. *Controllability*. We have the ability to change the conditions under which behavior is taking place and to produce the outcomes we predicted.[3]

Until recently, the four characteristics of a technology (predictability, measurability, understandability, and controllability) have been applied only by those individuals who have been with those responsible for technological systems such as machinery. Today, behavioral technology gives the behavioral engineer the advantages of those same four characteristics in examining human behavior. It is thus safe to say that we have a technology for dealing with human behavior—we can predict, measure, understand, and control human behavior.

In recent years, there has been a shift in the examination of human performance problems from the internal and philosophical approach to a more scientific approach. Because we now have this technology for dealing with human behavior, we can increase the amount of behavior in the organization that is supportive of organization goals, and we can decrease, minimize, or eliminate behavior that is nonsupportive of organizational goals.

THE ABC'S OF BEHAVIOR

If we are to develop a technology for analyzing behaviors, there are some basic principles worth knowing about. In school we learn our ABC's; it is not oversimplifying matters to suggest that there are ABC's of behavior as well.

1. *Antecedent.* The antecedent is what happens before the behavior occurs. It is a stimulus that provokes the behavior and is often in the form of cues from the environment including, but not limited to, something that someone else says or does, job routing cards, standards or objectives, notices on the employee bulletin board, machinery or equipment—any cues for employees suggesting they behave in a certain manner.

2. *Behavior.* This is something that the employee says or does on the job. It is usually an overt action such as filing a report, stamping a piece of paper, painting a part, coming to work on time—any one of a multitude of behaviors in which an employee engages in getting a job done.

3. *Consequence.* This is what happens after the employee behaves in a certain manner on the job. Consequences of behavior include bonuses, overtime pay, reprimands for excessive scrap, compliments for high-quality work, derision or compliments from fellow employees, or even attending a sales meeting in Honolulu.

From this basic model (see Figure 4.3), it is possible to analyze most human behavior. It is interesting to note the relationships between behavior, antecedent, and consequence. For instance, exam-

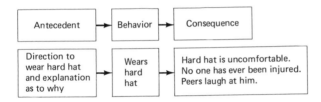

FIGURE 4.3   Basic model of behavior

ination of the antecedent can tell us a great deal about whether that behavior will occur at all. It does not, however, tell us much about whether that behavior will occur again.

Consider the case of an employee who is new to the job. Suppose that he is working for a contractor and his foreman welcomes him to the job, gives him a hard hat, and says that hard hats are very important. "We all wear hard hats around here for a couple of reasons. First, it is required by OSHA and second, the hard hat will keep a rivet from seriously injuring you, if a rivet were to fall from one of the upper stories and land on your head." This statement is the antecedent to the behavior of wearing a hard hat.

If all we knew about the job situation was this information, we could safely predict that the employee would wear the hard hat, at least for a while. Having instructed the employee on the importance of wearing a hard hat, showing him how to put it on, and making sure it is adjusted to the proper size, we might well leave him and walk away, secure in the knowledge that he will now wear his hard hat. Sure enough, we come by a couple of hours later and find him walking around with his hard hat firmly in place, thus protecting himself from the dangers that abound on the construction job. With our mind at ease, we can now go about our other duties. However, we have considered only two of the three elements in our basic analytical model for examining job behavior—the antecedent and the behavior. We note with satisfaction that the behavior is occurring at least during the first day of the job. We have not yet examined the consequences of wearing the hard hat, which determine whether the behavior will continue to occur.

Let's suppose that about a week later we go back and find, much to our chagrin and embarrassment, that the employee is no longer wearing his hard hat. Still concentrating only on the first two parts of our model (antecedent and behavior), we might conclude that he had forgotten our instruction, and we might again inform him why wearing the hard hat is important as well as giving him the correct techniques for adjusting hat size and making sure the hat is firmly in place. Once again, he acknowledges his understanding of our explanation, places his hard hat firmly in place, and marches off to perform his tasks. The next day we notice that by midmorning he is no longer wearing his hard hat.

We might conclude that although examining the behavior and what happens just before it is useful in predicting the behavior's first occurrence, it is perhaps not so useful in predicting whether that behavior will occur again. Pleased with our insightful look into human behavior, we would then begin to observe the consequences of that behavior. Examining this portion of the behavioral model, we note the following consequences:

1. It is August and very hot. The hard hat does not give much ventilation and can be extremely uncomfortable during the summer months.

2. Our new employee has found out that no one in the last three years has been injured while not wearing a hard hat, and he is willing to take a chance that he will not break that record.

3. We overheard two of his colleagues teasing him at lunchtime and asking whether he was going to put some stick-on flowers on his hard hat so he would look cute.

It begins to be clearer why the hard hat was removed (Figure 4.4). In examining the behavior and the consequences that relate to it, we can rather accurately predict whether the behavior will occur again. The general foreman can make the behavior start to occur, but he has a lot of work ahead of him to ensure that the employee will continue wearing the hard hat. The general foreman's directions are not enough to cause the behavior to be sustained beyond a few

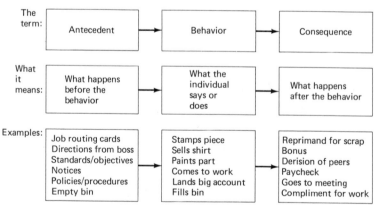

FIGURE 4.4   Antecedent-behavior-consequence relationships

hours. In fact, the consequences are such that the employee wears his hard hat only when the general foreman is present, he removes it whenever the foreman is away. The employee has the ability to relate certain consequences to certain cues, or antecedents, of behavior, and he behaves accordingly.

Using this basic model of antecedent, behavior, and consequence as a starting point, we may develop a model for analyzing human behavior. We must observe the individual in his or her job environment and examine those factors that affect the antecedent that leads to the behavior. We have to examine the behavior itself and the job situation in which the behavior takes place so that we can alter the elements that affect the behavior. We must also study the job situation to determine whether the behavior has positive consequences for the employee.

To develop trouble-shooting skills in analyzing human performance problems so that we will have a technology for dealing with these problems, we must stay within the parameters of the antecedent-behavior-consequence model. This model gives us the basis for examining human performance problems in the job situation. More importantly, using this behavioral model gives us a methodology for attacking problems that have previously defied definition and solution, such as "morale," "attitude," and "motivation." The model forces us to examine the individual in the job situation by asking the question in Table 4.1. If there is a performance problem,

---

TABLE 4.1 Performance Analysis

Antecedent
1. Does the employee know what is expected?
   Are the standards clear?
   Have they been communicated?
   Are they realistic?

Behavior
2. Can the behavior be performed?
   Could the employee do it if his or her life depended upon it?
   Does something prevent its occurrence?

Consequence
3. Are the consequences weighted in favor of performance?
4. Is there feedback about the consequences in relation to job performance?
   If yes, is the feedback immediate, specific, positive?
5. Are improvements being reinforced?
   Do we note improvements even though the improvement may still leave the employee below company standards?
   Is reinforcement specific?

---

we have to analyze that problem and develop solutions to it; but to do this we must first develop answers to each question. Then we can determine where the problem lies and find the solution to it.

An important note: if the manager is going to use this information, he should not ask the questions we have posed in Table 4.1 because he will only get opinions. Opinions are not very useful in building a sound technology for changing human behavior. What is essential is going into the organization and gathering information so that the manager can develop answers to the questions in Table 4.1 based upon factual data, not just employee opinions. This is a somewhat lengthy process but a more successful one. In answering questions, people often put into the answers their opinions, biases, and other irrelevant information. To develop a workable solution to human performance problems requires effective decision-making ability; a "good" decision based upon poor information is a lousy decision. If you want to avoid lousy decisions regarding human performance, don't ask the questions expressed here. Go gather your own information so that you can effectively develop your own answers.

With this model (see Figure 4.5) and these questions in mind, let's assume you are about to become sales manager for a firm that uses a distributor-retailer distribution system. As part of your job preparation, you ask your new boss about some of the problems he wants solved. Here is what you find out. As part of their regular duties, salespeople are required to submit weekly reports detailing the time they invest in making calls on each category of distributor during the week. This information is used by the home office as a basis for territory management and for determining marketing efforts, as well as for seeking areas where increased attention should be given. In theory, these reports enable management to make effective decisions in pricing, marketing, and product development. In practice, however, the reports are all but useless. Many of them have incorrect information; others are filled out improperly; and almost without exception, the sales staff fail to turn in their reports on time.

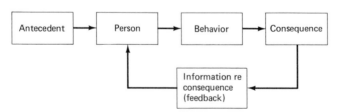

FIGURE 4.5   A model of behavioral analysis

As a result, the marketing effort often goes into the wrong territory. Products may be underpriced or overpriced, no one knows for sure; and managers are not sure that the sales force is calling on high-potential distributors to get the volume on high-margin products. They are never certain the penetration is all it should be. Investigation finds that every so often, the present sales manager sent a blistering memo to the salespeople berating them for the inaccuracy and tardiness of their reports. For a couple of weeks after sending one of those memos, reports came in looking pretty neat and on time, but this situation never lasted for more than a few weeks. The previous sales manager was a pretty hard-working guy. When asked about the reporting problems, he said, "I've got 11 salesmen in the field and not one of those clowns hands in his report on time. Because they are geographically so far away, I can't send them back to get them corrected so I do the best I can to patch them up and make sense out of them." If the questions in Table 4.1 are used as a method of tackling this particular performance problem, it can be approached by determining which variable or combination of variables has broken down. The problem could be in the antecedent, the behavior itself or in the consequence. Asking our questions, results in these answers:

Antecedent: Does the individual know what is expected?
- The salespeople know they are to turn in good reports. They know the dates, the dates are realistic, and they have been communicated to the sales staff on numerous occasions.

Behavior: Can the behavior be performed?
- The salespeople know almost everything there is to know about submitting good reports.
- Although they know what to write, the salespeople don't know how to write it. There is no model or sample report to guide their writing of the information so that it will be useful at headquarters.

Consequence: Are the consequences positive or performing correctly? Is there good feedback? Are improvements being noticed and reinforced?
- The sales staffs have never been exactly sure why their reports have been unacceptable; the former sales manager never sent them photocopies of the revisions he made in their reports.
- There is less punishment for submitting late reports than in getting them in on time. The sales manager returns incomplete reports for correction when they are submitted on time. If reports are turned in late, the sales manager corrects them himself, spar-

ing the sales staff the tedious job of correcting the reports—a reward for slipshod work.
• Salespeople who turn in accurate reports on time never hear about it; salespeople who turn in inaccurate reports late never receive any feedback about it. The only actual feedback, or consequence (according to our model), is that every several months, the blistering memo goes out berating everyone for late and inaccurate reports.

Our model as shown in Figure 4.5 has important implications for today's manager; in the context of this model, the manager's job can be defined as encompassing these specific responsibilities:

Specifying the needed behaviors to accomplish the job.
Setting the standards of performance related to those behaviors.
Seeing that the cues (antecedents) for the job behavior are clear.
Seeing that nothing interferes with the task being performed so that the relationship between the antecedent and the behavior is not broken.
Arranging some positive feedback as a consequence for the correct behavior.
Seeing that this necessary feedback is imparted to the employee.
Reinforcing improvements in employee performance.

Within the context of the elements discussed so far, we can construct the model shown in Figure 4.6. This model encompasses the basic concept of antecedent-behavior-consequence examined earlier (those parts of the model that are related in the first seven steps) and combines it with what we will examine in the remaining chapters of the book (steps 8 through 13). Let's briefly run an example through the model so that we can see how it might work in a job situation (see Figure 4.6).

Step 1 is to identify a potential performance improvement area. Maybe it is in quality control, manufacturing, warehousing, expense, cost containment, sales, or invoicing. Single out an area. Let's use quality control as our target area and let the project expand from there. Step 2 is to identify the present performance level in this area. We will have to establish certain specific measurements of performance and identify the present performance level for each of these. They may include, for instance, rejects, reworks, and scrap. Incidentally, the curious thing about pinpointing present performance level in my experience in working with wholesalers, retailers, manufacturers, financial institutions, and a variety of other organizations is

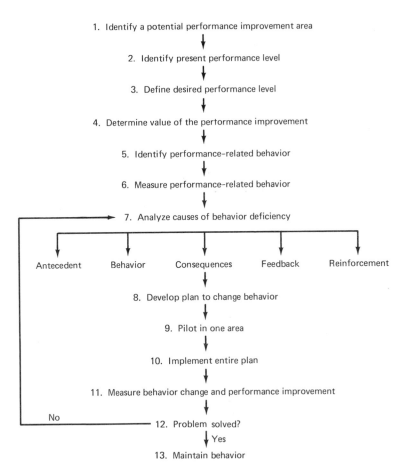

1. Identify a potential performance improvement area

2. Identify present performance level

3. Define desired performance level

4. Determine value of the pertormance improvement

5. Identify performance-related behavior

6. Measure performance-related behavior

7. Analyze causes of behavior deficiency

Antecedent   Behavior   Consequences   Feedback   Reinforcement

8. Develop plan to change behavior

9. Pilot in one area

10. Implement entire plan

11. Measure behavior change and performance improvement

No

12. Problem solved?   Yes

13. Maintain behavior

FIGURE 4.6   Performance analysis model

that the present performance level is never exactly what we think it is. An important thing to remember in the application of this technology is that it is not enough to accept the performance level you get from reports as the basis for developing your behavior-change program. Investigate beyond the reports. One firm with whom we worked, for example, asked us to undertake some projects in the area of quality control and inventory shrinkage. One of the areas within quality control they were concerned about was scrap, which was running on the reports at 3.05 percent in plant A and 5.9 percent in Plant B. The overall goal had been established at approximately 1.8 percent. In Plant A, we found that scrap dollars as a percentage of direct labor dollars were running at 5.1 percent; at Plant B, scrap dollars as a percentage of direct labor dollars were running at 13.4 percent. We determined these figures through a study conducted after hours that included analysis of scrap tickets, identification and evaluation of items found in dumpsters, and untagged and unrecorded scrap found under machines or underneath the offall. In short, rather than reporting scrap, people were ignoring it or in some cases deliberately hiding it. With this in mind, our next step, step 3, was to define the desired performance level. Some standards were already set, but based upon the identification of the present performance level, it was determined that the standards were unrealistically tight. By plant and by department (press, milling, welding, etc.), desired performance levels for scrap, rework, and inventory shrinkage were identified.

With the difference between present performance level and desired performance level established, numbers could now be plugged into our formula

$$\left(\text{value} = \frac{\text{annual return} - \text{ongoing cost}}{\text{initial cost}} \right)$$

to determine the total value of potential performance improvement (step 4). The total potential savings from the project were projected to be $923,500 and the ongoing costs were projected to be $3,000. The initial cost associated with the project including analysis of the performance problems, employees training in using the techniques of behavioral analysis, and aid in implementing and monitoring the project to ensure that the action steps were working as planned was $47,000. The value of the performance improvement was set at

$$19 \left(\frac{[923,500 - 3,000]}{47,000} \right) = 19.5851.$$

With such a payoff in mind, step 5 was to identify specific behaviors related to the desired performance. These included, but were not limited to, reporting all scrap, getting first piece inspection, identifying and taking care of scrap within the same shift, placing the scrap in designated areas, and sending reports back to the operator who caused the rework to be necessary.

Some of these behaviors were already occurring and some were not (step 6). Each was measured and current levels identified.

Step 7 was to determine which of the primary causes of behavior deficiency was preventing the necessary or desired behavior on the job. Based on this analysis, a series of actions were undertaken that constituted the plan for eliciting the behavior required on the job. (We will look at the analysis of each of these areas in succeeding chapters.) Some of these steps were implemented right away (step 8) and others were piloted, depending upon the degree of certainty and predictability each of these steps had. After the bugs had been worked out of the piloted areas, the plan was implemented fully in both plants. Measurement and evaluation (step 11) of the performance improvement have been on an ongoing basis. In a couple of departments, there were initially some problems with the performance level (step 12), so the efforts are recycled through the model starting with analyzing the causes of behavior deficiency in those particular departments. Annualized savings were presently running at approximately $440,000 a year. To see how savings of that magnitude were realized, let's turn to each of the potential problem areas (antecedent, job behavior, consequences, feedback, and reinforcement) and see how each of these in turn affects human behavior on the job and how steps might be developed to make the necessary changes.

5

Objectives as Antecedents to Behavior

EXPECTATIONS AND STANDARDS: ANTECEDENTS TO BEHAVIOR

Members of organizations, although they may be very qualified, often fail to perform with maximum effectiveness just because they do not know the results that are expected of them. They are unaware of the goals sought, the purpose of their work, or how effectively they are achieving those goals. In your own organization, try this test just to illustrate the point:

1. Take a sheet of paper and list the answers to the following questions about one of your key subordinates:
   a. What are the major result areas in his job this year?
   b. For each of these result areas, what specific results do you expect at the end of this year?

2. Ask that subordinate to answer these same questions about his or her job without having seen your notes.

3. Compare the responses with your own responses. Chances are you and your subordinate will agree on only about 75 percent of the answers.

This matched interviewing is widespread in all kinds of firms. The average difference between the boss and his or her subordinate is usually 25 percent. The implications of this are serious. If subordinate and superior do not agree specifically on what constitutes the subordinate's job (in terms of results), bad performance may not be due to the subordinate's weakness in the job but to his or her not knowing what the job is.

EXPECTATIONS AND BEHAVIOR

Mismatches like this occur for many reasons. First, there is a lack of communication. Studies by many communications experts show that as a message moves down through the channels of an organization, it becomes garbled and confused. The president of the firm says he would be very pleased if everyone contributed to the United Fund drive. By the time that message has moved down through the vice president to the general manager, plant manager, superintendent, and foreman, it comes across as, "If you guys don't contribute to United Fund, you are going to be out on the street." Some of this message garbling or misrepresenting is to be expected, but much of it can be eliminated by using proper communications techniques designed to remove filters in the communications system and ensure that what is said in the beginning is what is heard at the end.

A second reason for the mismatch in results accomplished by the employee and results desired by the manager is the failure to integrate standards, goals, and expectations across organizational lines. Manufacturing and sales, for example, impact each others' operations, but often their goals aren't integrated. A case in point: in the mid-1960s, one of the automotive manufacturers discovered, belatedly, that within the organization marketing and manufacturing were not checking expectations with each other. At a time when a particular model was selling rather poorly, manufacturing was making modifications in their tooling and scheduling to reduce production of that model. Unbeknown to them, their counterparts in marketing were busy designing a special campaign geared to bring sales of the model back up to previous levels. The marketing campaign was successful. Sales started climbing. Unfortunately, backlog climbed even more rapidly. Orders for the model poured in the front door of the firm but manufacturing could not fill all the orders. Furthermore, they no longer had sufficient equipment or employees to produce the large numbers of that particular model now required to meet the needs of the marketing campaign.

Because of an oversight, no one in marketing had informed manufacturing of the new advertising and sales campaign. In this case, certain behaviors were required of the manufacturing department but it couldn't perform those behaviors and produce the cars needed. In the behavior model that we examined earlier (antecedent-behavior-consequences), it is with the antecedent in this instance that the performance system broke down. Manufacturing did not know what expectations were placed on them because of a breakdown in communications and a failure within the organization to share new objectives and action plans across functional lines. In this instance no organizational cue started the behavior. Needless to say, the impact felt by the entire company, not just the manufacturing and marketing departments, was enormous and caused significant problems in the areas of customer relations, production scheduling, and dealer relations. Organizational planning has to cross department lines.

Another cause of the mismatch with which we are concerned is lack of knowledge about what we expect from employees in their job performance. Because we are unable to be specific with employees about our job expectations of them, we often focus instead on irrelevant characteristics (in an attempt to get someone back on the track). To motivate a wayward employee, the boss seizes upon something that seems appropriate to the problem at hand.

"The problem with you, Sarah, is that you are not production-oriented. If we are going to keep our costs down in manufacturing, we all have to work hard at it." The fact that Sarah is a copywriter in the advertising department does not deter us from giving advice that is inappropriate. Cost control in manufacturing, we naively think, applies to just about everybody in the company, and if we could just get Sarah interested in it, it would probably be good for her too. Sarah, of course, is confused by all this concern with manufacturing costs; she would rather work on advertising copy, but she promises the boss to give it the old college try. The net effect of this information on Sarah's job performance: nothing.

Another possible cause of the mismatch is that we don't articulate our desires. "If you are going to succeed in marketing, Don, you will need more perseverance." It's up to Don to translate "perseverance" into specific job behaviors that will improve the company's sales effort. What the vice president of marketing meant was that the field sales force would have to do a better job of analyzing its call reports and focusing their efforts on high-potential distributors.

The odds are stacked against both the boss and Don in this situation, because Don can interpret "perseverance" in a variety of ways, including an order to work longer hours, call on more distributors, sell a more complete product line, increase penetration of higher-margin products, send in more reports, submit needed reports, cut travel expense, reduce telephone expense, cut entertainment expense, spend less time with distributors' sales staff, spend more time with distributors' sales staff, use a new "rock 'em–sock 'em" sales technique, or not use a new "rock 'em–sock 'em" sales technique. The probability of Don's grasping the specific action desired is not very high. Additionally, if the boss puts a lot of pressure on Don, Don may try all the options that he sees as viable and let some other aspect of his job fall below standard, such as recruiting and hiring a new salesperson—activities that the boss may wish to be maintained at their present level of effectiveness.

If we want Don to perform his job correctly, that is, if we specifically want him to increase sales of high-margin items, that's what we must articulate to him. It is not enough to tell him he needs more perseverance and that he has to keep his shoulder to the wheel.

Of the four possible reasons for the mismatch of communications (what we want and what we get), lack of knowledge about the job performance we expect and failure to articulate what we want accounts for most of the performance deficiency.

Some managers argue that it is impossible to articulate what they want because the job is "nebulous," "difficult to define." Conversations with these managers are always interesting and usually go something like this. Says the manager, "You don't understand; we are different. The type of work we do around here is very unusual and identifying results on the job here is extremely difficult. In fact, it borders on impossible because we are really dealing with creative geniuses; you can't measure genius."

"Say, that sounds very interesting," comes the reply. "Could you tell me exactly what it is you work on in this creative process?"

"Well, we work on a variety of things including basic research design and the transfer of technology from one product area to another."

"Yes, I can see where that would be difficult to work with. Tell me this, how many people are there on your staff?"

"Well, in total there are about 45 people in the department."

"Are some of those individuals better performers than others?"

"Oh, yeah, we have four or five clearly top performers, one or two who aren't very good, and the others who are pretty good."

"Well, are any of them ready for promotion?"

"Yes," the manager replies.

"Have you ever promoted anybody out of this department to another job?"

"Yes, we promote one or two people a year."

"Has anybody ever been fired from this department?"

"Yes, just last year we had to let three people go for poor performance."

"Let me ask you this three-part question. What was there in the performance of the people you had to let go that required you to let them go? What was there in the performance of the people you promoted? When you gave pay raises, what made you think they were deserved?"

"Well, that's kind of tough to identify. You see, we are in sort of a unique business here and the creative process is different from working with other jobs."

At this point it's back to go and we sing the refrain again. Such conversations are nonsense, of course. People do get fired every day; people get promoted every day; and people get pay raises every day in all kinds of organizations. The reasons they are fired, promoted, or receive pay raises are generally due to something they have done or failed to do on the job. It is not that there are no standards and expectations. It is not that there is a unique situation with this company. Simply stated, the problem is the unwillingness of a manager to confront his expectations of employees and to articulate them to staff members. Every employee should be guided in spending his or her time. Employees shouldn't have unanswered questions about what is expected of them. They should have a framework within which to work. When an employee's targets have been well identified and designed, his or her contribution to the performance and profitability of the entire organization increases significantly.

THE IMPORTANCE OF OUTLINING
SPECIFIC JOB EXPECTATIONS

As a system of leadership within an organization, a results-orientation that outlines specific job expectations is of substantial benefit and unquestionable value. First, it is based upon both corporate and individual performance. By specifying specific accomplishments that are needed, company goals and objectives of individuals within the organization are spelled out. Everyone moves in the same direction toward the accomplishment of all organizational objectives. In Figure 5.1, for example, a corporate goal related to earnings per share translates itself several times as it works down through the different levels of the organization. At the very top of the organization, it is expressed in terms of increasing earnings per share. At the divisional general manager level, the same objective translates into return on investment (ROI) and moves to the plant level and is translated into unit cost. By the time it gets down to the department foreman, the same expectations are outlined in terms of rework cost. as a percentage of direct labor dollars.

At each level of the organization, there are specific job behaviors that each individual will have to perform if goals are to be met. Each individual in the chain (president, general manager, superintendent, foreman) has to develop specific action plans to ensure that the targets are met. If the targets are not being met, the behaviors associated with that target are probably not being performed. The supervisor of the nonperforming employee must begin the coaching process, clarifying goals and showing what behavior is required. Let's assume, for example, that the foreman is not meeting his rework objective. Although it will be quite some time before that makes a significant impact on the earnings per share objectives, the time to begin to nip such problems is when they begin.

It is the job of the superintendent to sit down with the foreman

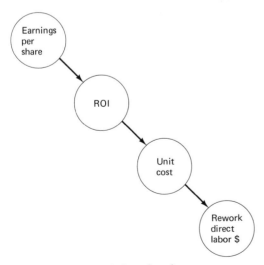

FIGURE 5.1   Translation of goals

and go over not only the objective but also each of the specific behaviors required of him by the action plan to ensure accomplishment of that objective. It could be that only one step is being omitted simply because the foreman isn't aware that it's part of the necessary behavior pattern. He might, for example, be newly appointed and not be aware that operations are supposed to check one piece in 20 to ensure that it meets standards. The superintendent serves as a coach ensuring that the specific behaviors necessary to reach the objective are communicated and reinforced by the foreman.

Let's look at the standards and targets to see how they work and how they might be set up to improve employee performance. First, these standards provide an employee with yardsticks by which to judge his or her performance. They provide an end target toward which the employee can aim behavioral patterns on the job. The word "target" is an apt one. A rifleman with an identifiable target stands a better chance of hitting it than one who has a partially hidden target or one that is continually moving. All three of these riflemen stand a better chance of hitting their targets than someone with no target at all—no direction in which to aim. To draw the analogy further, the rifleman with no target, no idea which direction to aim, actually ends up endangering other people. This is also the case with an employee who has no target. He or she may head off in the wrong direction, thus unknowingly damaging other people in the organization or hindering the performance of other departments.

This lack of direction can manifest itself in several ways. An employee, for example, who has no clearly specified target in the area of product quality might well lean toward the target of production quantity. This would have a severe impact on other operations further down the line. The saying, "A lot of what you are producing is junk," is expressed more often than we would like to think and in more organizations than we would like to consider, including hospitals, manufacturing firms, educational institutions, and government units. People often wonder why this is so. Our mismatched communications problem rears its ugly head in many places. Setting clearly defined, understandable targets for employees in conjunction with organizational targets helps overcome this mismatch.

SOURCES OF INFORMATION FOR JOB STANDARDS

Job standards relate to employee performance. They can be developed from a variety or a combination of sources. One possibility is to develop a flow chart and then attach job expectations to each point on the chart. Let's take, for example, the job of mailroom clerk or messenger. Assume that the mailroom handles three types of mail: incoming mail, outgoing mail, and interdepartmental mail. Here, we consider only outgoing mail, but a similar flow chart can be developed for both incoming and interdepartmental mail. As we can see from Figure 5.2, several areas for developing standards exist.

Job standards might relate to the length of time between receiving the outgoing mail in the mailroom and delivering it to the U.S. Postal Service. Other standards can also be established about the correct amount of postage and use of correct zip codes.

A second way to develop standards for the outgoing mail staff is to base job behaviors upon an analysis matrix. In Figure 5.3, we can break down the elements of a job and assign them to individual personnel within a department. For each job element it is possible to develop a standard. For instance, the amount of time required to send interdepartmental mail from one department to another can be cited, and the average number of pieces of interdepartmental mail handled per man-hour can be suggested. With the matrix example, each job

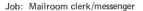

Job: Mailroom clerk/messenger

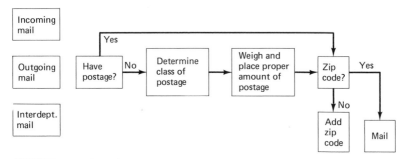

FIGURE 5.2   Flow chart analysis

Part of organization: mailroom

Activities	Personnel		
	Joe	Bob	Hazel
Incoming sort			X
stack			X
deliver	X		
Outgoing pick up		X	
check add.		X	
check post.			X
post office	X		

FIGURE 5.3   Matrix analysis

element can be assigned specifically to one individual. This allows pinpointing of the job element and assignment of it to a specific individual within the department.

A third possibility for developing information regarding job standards is simply to use engineering job standards. This task should be performed by industrial engineers. There are a variety of techniques available to industrial engineers in setting job standards, including measured day work, synthetic standards, or a combination of both. This approach is used most often in plant work, and most manufacturing facilities use some type of job standard for their production jobs. Whichever method is used, the use of job standards in production has proven to be very beneficial in identifying specific job elements, in attaching a necessary time to complete each job segment to that element, and then in totaling the completion times to determine the appropriate amount of time required to complete that task. Most organizations attach such standards to the job routing card so that the individual machine operator, for example, knows how much time he is given to complete each piece of work.

Since the mid- to late 1960s, industrial engineers have also moved out of the plant and into other areas of organizations. Organizations with large clerical operations have found that industrial engineers can be of use in determining the amount of time required to process paperwork as well as the most efficient movement system for that paper. Additionally, industrial engineers have been used in the health care field, initially to determine how many meals to put on a cart to maximize the number of meals delivered in a given period, while at the same time ensuring that meals are maintained at least at a minimum temperature. More recently, however, health care organizations have used industrial engineering firms in concert with architects to design not only operational systems but also the basic layout of hospitals so that the work of the organization can flow smoothly.

Past job history also often provides information about job standards. Just because some level of performance has occurred in the past does not necessarily mean that that's the level of performance we wish to repeat in the future or that is possible to have in the future. In the absence of other information, however, past history gives us a useful base from which to start establishing job standards. In addition to providing useful information on where we have been, historical information can help us make decisions and determine performance improvement areas for the future.

For example, accounting information can be compared with corresponding reports from previous years or with statements from other firms in the same industry to determine whether performance in a given area is adequate.

Selecting historical information as a basis for determining job standards does not mean we should accept that information without checking it thoroughly. To be used properly as a basis for determining job standards, there must be an "apple-to-apple" comparison. For example, if rework as a percentage of total labor dollars has been running at 3.2 percent in Plant A in the past, we should check that figure against other comparable items before we accept it as standard, including other plants we own that produce similar products, an industry average, other plants of a similar nature in our own geographical region, and the economic conditions prevailing when the data were gathered. We should also be careful that these comparisons do not contain extraneous information. If, for example, our rework percentage is running at 3.4 percent and that of another plant at 1.9 percent, this does not mean our standard should automatically be 1.9 percent. Accounting items may be included in our 3.4 percent that are not included in the 1.9 percent; these items should be discounted when determining the standard. By the same token, just because our rework percentage is 3.4 percent and someone else's is 4.1 percent does not necessarily mean we are doing a good job. We might have failed to include some items that they are including; we might have dissimilar product lines; we might be working with different materials; or any of another host of variables. Thus, while job history provides a useful perspective, we must make sure that any comparison with other organizations is on an apples-to-apples basis. Then we must integrate that information into our own thinking, our own personal situation, and in our decision-making process come up with a realistic standard.

THE USE OF PERFORMANCE INDICATORS IN ESTABLISHING STANDARDS OF PERFORMANCE

Job results around which standards are established are measured in terms of four areas:

1. Quantity—how many someone produces.
2. Quality—how well he or she does it.
3. Timeliness—how long it takes.
4. Costs—how much it costs.

Each of these provides useful information for setting up standards for different types of jobs. In a few instances, a job area may not have all four of these performance indicators but will certainly have most of them. These four measurement tools—quality, quantity, timeliness, and costs—in turn, can be used to generate other performance indicators that are useful for the job under discussion. Below are some examples to help you identify useful indicators.

Units produced per shift
Applications processed per week
Grievances per quarter   = Quantity
Home runs hit

Programing errors
Error rate
Rejection ratio   = Quality
Batting average

Percentage of on time departures
Percentage of budget reports turned in on time   = Timeliness
Grievances handled in two working days or passed up
Processing time

Percentage of deviation from
   budget
$ cost of downtime   = Cost
Processing costs
Average crew size

Table 5.1 is a list of indicators generated in management workshops by looking at the areas of quantity, quality, timeliness, and costs. For an interesting project, identify those indicators in Table 5.1 that you feel relate to one of your key subordinates. Next to each performance indicator, write down the performance level you think appropriate for that job. Place that sheet of paper in the desk drawer. Now take the list of sample indicators to your same key subordinate and without letting that individual see what you identified as the critical indicators and standards, ask the subordinate to repeat the same process. Chances are you will agree neither on the priority of the indicators nor on the expected results. You have just done on your own the interview described earlier in this chapter.

Standards should also be output-related rather than activity-related. Output is the completed work left behind when the employee

TABLE 5.1   A Practice Set

Pick out one of your subordinates and place his/her name above.

Return on investment	Tardiness
Production volume	Absenteeism
Quality level	Turnaround time
Cost of rework	Number vendor contracts
Scrap rate	Unit cost of purchases
Direct costs	Vendor research
Indirect costs	Percentage of and dollar commit-
Budget	ment to dispersements
Safety	Purchases vs. purchase expense
Housekeeping	Learning curve
Suggestions	Milestones for projects
Grievances	Vendors performance against
Employee development	requisitions
Schedules	Training hours and cost ratios
Sales volume	Number training completions
Cost of sales	Coaching (i.e., development against
Gross margin	specified criteria)
Mark ups	Floor space
Mark downs	Number of experiments
Reports	Drawings released
Crew size	Engineering change requests
Operating cost per unit	Reliability/cost ratios
Service requests	Comparative cost estimates
Salary cost per unit	Predesign research costs
Overhead per unit	Tangible production improvements
Receiving and shipping cost per unit	(rates, rejects, etc.)
Containers-pilferage-damage	Response time
Turnover	Flow time
Complaints	Cost/value ratios
Cost savings	Customer acceptance
Commitments	Analytical errors
College recruiting	Average cost per analysis
Quotas	Operational improvements

goes home, not the process by which that work is completed. "Installing engines," for example, is work process, but work output is "engine installed." There is a small semantic difference between the two terms but a very important practical difference. Filing reports is an on-going process; reports filed is a completed process. Job standards should concentrate on output, not on the process by which outputs are achieved. Table 5.2 gives examples of processes and outputs.

TABLE 5.2   **Examples of Processes and Outputs**

Processes	Outputs
Selling	Dollar volume sold
Helping	Yield
Making	Units produced
Coaching	Number of promotable subordinates
Cleaning	Bacterial count
Cross-selling	Number of customers with more than one service
Washing	Linen costs per patient day

Work process tells us only what occurs on the job while work output tells us what is accomplished on the job and is much more useful in determining the level of performance required within that job situation.

A final method for developing job standards is the discussion between boss and subordinate. This process is often part of the four areas discussed above, although it can be used as the sole basis for developing job standards. It is most common in the middle-management range or between a department head and nonsupervisory but highly professional employees; for example, between the department head of accounting and some of the key professionals within the accounting department. It is also a useful tool in developing standards when job conditions change or when the organization changes. In these last two instances, change usually means some type of parameter modification that affects the job performance or the specific standards associated with a job.

CHARACTERISTICS OF GOOD STANDARDS

If a standard is to be a useful guide for the job performer, it must be specific, realistic, and sensitive to change; fit the requirements of the observable job; and describe the terms of job outputs. Let's see how each of these terms can be used to develop good standards.

First, consider specificity. In our rush to establish job standards, we could turn to our secretary and say, "I realize one of the areas in which I have been deficient as your supervisor is failing to communicate to you exactly what I expect in terms of job standards. Therefore, I would like to tell you at this time some of the standards I see as being part of your job responsibility. I have only had time to work on two areas, but I will complete the others and we can discuss them as soon as I complete the information. The two areas in which I have developed some standards are telephone practices and typing. As far as the telephone goes, the standard I would like you to keep in mind is to be prompt and courteous in answering my phone. In typing, I expect you to do a good job in a neat and efficient manner." Very self-satisfied with the efforts to communicate these standards, I can sit back and relax now that my secretary knows exactly what is expected.

However, the result of this conversation is twofold: first, my secretary probably doesn't know anymore than she did before about what is expected of her except that we're concerned about two things: telephone and typing. She then begins to put a lot of effort into these tasks not knowing exactly where she is to expend the rest of her effort. Hopefully, she would show that the communication is two-way and turn to us and say, "That sounds like a good start. It would, however, help me a great deal if I knew specifically what you meant. For example, chief, in the area of general typing, exactly what do you mean by 'neat and prompt?' " To this very insightful question, she would probably get this response: "Specifically, what I mean in terms of general typing is that there be no errors on corrected copy in either spelling or grammar. There should be no physical corrections on corrected copy. You should be able to type from either dictation or longhand. The work should be completed by the time I request it, and everything should be proofread before you give it to me to sign or before you send it out to some other department such as printing.

"As to your question regarding the telephone, I see two specific areas which need work. I think your phone should be answered within three rings. Your personal conversations should be limited to no more than 25 minutes per day with a maximum of 10 minutes in any one conversation. As to my phone, I think it should be answered by the second ring when I am not in the office. The caller should be asked if he would like to leave a message and he should also know when I will be back in the office or where I may be reached. If I am in the office, I think you should answer the phone after the third ring and explain to the caller that I have someone in my office and ask if I can return the call at a later time." With all this new information and more specific information, my secretary can then perform her job in a far more satisfactory manner, which really meets the standards we feel are important to be met in her job.

The second characteristic of setting good job standards is that it be realistic. Reality-based standards are much more useful not only in evaluating job performance but also, and more importantly, in establishing a basis for operational information. Too many of us try to establish standards that are unrealistically high "to put some stretch into the job" or try to establish objectives that are unrealistically low to "give the person a chance to succeed." In our work with various organizations, we have found that neither of these approaches works well. In fact, we find that a combination of both approaches, a realistic approach, works best. Reality is not a single number. Reality is usually a combination of numbers based upon a whole series of variables that affect job performance. In manufacturing, for example, an average hourly production rate between 110 and 120 might be considered satisfactory. The individual that falls between these numbers is meeting the standard. A production supervisor can thus be told one of the areas of job standards for his position is the rate of production. We expect that you will probably average between 110 and 120 units an hour. Not only does this give the individual some measure of flexibility in meeting the requirements of the job; it also meets both of the conditions stated above. First, it gives the individual a level of performance (110) that is relatively easy to meet and thus providing for a feeling of success on the job; second, it gives the individual a stretch target (120 units per hour) that motivates the individual by building some challenge into the job.

The third characteristic of setting good job standards is fitting the requirements to the job. Telling the production manager that one of his job standards is built around advertising expense as a percentage of sales, and that acceptable expenses should be between 2.8 and 3.4 percent of sales does not do very much to fit the requirements of his particular job, unless the production manager also happens to be responsible for the advertising budget. A primary purpose of good job standards is to provide managers with information that is useful in directing the fulfillment of their particular responsibilities. If the standard does not fit the requirements of that job, it is of little or no use as a management or performance improvement tool. Job standards should be applied to areas either under the direct control or the direct influence of the individual responsible for meeting those standards. Thus, an airport manager, for example, might have a standard related to on-time departures (that is, the percentage of planes that leave the gate within 10 minutes of scheduled departure time). This number fits the requirements of the job and should allow for a number of variables such as weather that may affect performance. By ensuring that each standard fits the particular requirements of the job, it is possible to build standards that each individual can meet; then the department meets its standards and, as a result, the entire company meets its earnings-per-share projection.

Finally, standards must be observable. It does no good to say that a job standard is proper unless we can observe whether it is being met. Observation might be through X-ray, destructive testing on a sample basis, or some other method, but if a job standard is to be useful to a manager in determining performance improvement areas, it must be observable whether or not the standard has been met.

Establishing unobservable job standards is analogous to telling an Olympic runner that the standard for getting into the finals of the 100-meter dash is the ability to run 100 meters in 11 seconds. Having communicated this standard to the runner, promptly remove all timing devices from the stadium in which he is to compete. If the individual runs 100 meters, there is no way of timing the performance. How foolhardy not to be able to observe and measure the runner's performance! Although we can certainly determine variations that are significantly out of line (like running it in 22 seconds), there is no observable way of determining whether the runner has met the 11-second standard. Similar situations occur on the job when we can't measure or observe whether standards are being met. We can say to someone that the standard in a particular job is the turnaround time (that is, the amount of time between receiving something in the office and getting it out of the office in three working days). If we have no tracking mechanism for determining whether that turnaround took place within three days, we do not have an observable, measurable standard.

6

Training as a Behavior-Change Agent

Training has not always been considered an agent of behavior change. Early businessmen believed any training other than the most elementary was unnecessary. Not until the manpower shortage of World War I became critical did this position change.

World War I brought the first changes. Although these changes were not revolutionary, they were important because they were the first step in the evolution of training and development as we know it today. As industry geared up to meet the war needs and many skilled employees joined the military, industry was forced to train people to fill these gaps. From this modest beginning, the field quickly returned to its former state after demobilization. As the Depression years dawned, lines outside employment offices grew longer each day. Training faded into memory and constant hiring and firing once again became the norm.

As World War II came into view, industry began tooling up. The new war placed previously unheard-of demands upon the American economy. With the bulk of its work force in uniform, there were few places left to turn for skilled help. In fact, there was little skilled help available. Out of the woodwork came 13,000,000 untrained, unskilled, and inexperienced workers. The vast majority of these were trained by Job Instruction Techniques, a method still used today. This previously untrained, unskilled, and inexperienced work force turned out a supply of war goods reaching from the factory door to the four corners of the world. Supervisors were trained under a program sponsored by the United States Department of Education (Engineering, Science, and Management War Training). Training had become big business, the illegitimate child had finally been adopted as a legitimate activity of business organizations, one that paid off on the profit and loss statement.

The end of World War II might have brought an end to the sudden reenchantment with training. After all, the training star had risen once already, only to be quickly retired with the lean years of the Depression. Such was not the case. In fact, just the opposite occurred—training received more emphasis in the postwar years than it had during the war; not for all the right reasons, perhaps, but it was emphasized nevertheless.

An unnoticed problem had developed in industry. The Depression and World War II had in combination created an unusual situation. Much of top management was approaching retirement age, and there were no younger managers to fill these positions. No management training had occurred during the Depression, and the war had taken many younger people who might have gained experience by the trial and error method in industry. The need for skilled labor and management personnel was greater than ever before. If industrial expansion was to be carried on, then accelerated training programs were the only answer. Industry could no longer depend on the long process of learning by many years of experience. Many of the skills that had to be developed had no previous pattern. Training was necessary on all levels in many business organizations. Methods had to be developed to impart this training as rapidly as possible.[1]

TRAINING EFFECTIVENESS

Today, training in business and industry is big business. Estimates of the amount invested by industry in the development of human resources range from $3 billion to $35 billion a year, depending upon whom you consult and what figures they include or refer to. Education of all types is the fastest growing industry in the United States; continuing education is the fastest growing segment of this industry. In the right situation, training is an excellent method of changing employee behavior. It should be, however, the last used and the least used method in changing behavior. Unfortunately, it is usually the first used and the most often used. In part, this is because of the lack of concern for the effectiveness of employee training programs.

In the development of effective management practices, there is a difference between effectiveness (doing the right things) and efficiency (doing things right or correctly). Much the same is true in the development of training programs. There is a high payoff for efficiency (learning the competencies correctly), but there is a higher payoff for effectiveness (learning the right competencies). Most literature dealing with training focuses upon the best methods for transferring information from the body of knowledge through the medium selected to the student, who then carries this information to the "real world," or job situation.

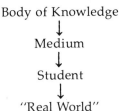

This is an important process for it deals with the efficiency of education, finding the right method for the transfer of knowledge. Later in this chapter, we comment on different methodologies and which of these is most efficient for the transfer of knowledge. This emphasis, however, overlooks the more important issue of the *effectiveness* of the education, making sure that we are teaching the right things. In terms of employee training, it may well be more economical to spend $500,000 to analyze in depth the required competencies or behaviors that are required on the job and to provide training in them for the right people than to provide training to all employees in all competencies. There is, after all, no point in teaching well that which should not be taught at all.

This concept of effectiveness deals with the first step in designing a training program for analyzing the behavioral deficiency of the prospective student. A simple way of examining this deficiency is to list the behaviors required on the job and subtract from it the behaviors the prospective student already has; that equals our deficiency.

That's simple, you say. All you have to do is look at what prospective employees can accomplish and what they need to accomplish, then teach them the difference. That will enable them to accomplish whatever you want in their job.

For example, safety specialists in a large food chain determined that back injuries sustained by store and warehouse employees resulted in an annual expense of $1 million, which included insurance premiums, lost time, and training replacements. Investigation revealed that the injuries were caused by improper lifting procedures. The action of the safety specialists in response to this problem illustrates the application of behavioral analysis as a technique whose effectiveness can be measured in economic terms. The process used in deciding to apply behavioral analysis is an example of carefully diagnosing the problem rather than choosing one solution without examining alternatives.

When the safety director first asked the training representative to do something about the number of injuries, it seemed that the solution would be to develop a new course on lifting to replace the existing course, which included pamphlets, films, and lifting practice. But instead of accepting this initial idea, the safety director analyzed the problem of injuries to make certain that something other than lack of knowledge of lifting procedures was not the cause. He first asked whether the existing course really failed to reach employees to lift properly. He observed that employees were able to lift correctly at the conclusion of the course but they didn't always do this on the job. Next, he considered whether the method of lifting taught in the existing course was incorrect. Since injuries had not occurred when employees used the recommended lifting procedures, the safety director and the training representative decided that those procedures were probably adequate. They determined that the real problem was getting the employees to apply at all times the lifting procedures they had been taught.

This analysis of what had to be done was followed by an analysis of how to do it. The existing system of supervisors' reprimanding employees for lifting improperly had changed employee behavior little if at all; therefore, the idea of a stricter system of reprimands was rejected. Instead, the company decided to try reinforcing proper lifting: that is, supervisors of store and warehouse employees whose jobs involved lifting were instructed to praise employees who lifted properly.

The prospective students, then, were the supervisors of the employees whose jobs involved lifting, rather than the employees themselves. The company decided to teach behavioral conditioning as a management technique by a programed course.

The course dealt specifically with the lifting problem and taught little of the general theory of behavioral conditioning. The program stressed examples of what to say in particular situations when a worker lifted correctly. It was written at a level easily understood by the supervisors, who averaged an eleventh-grade education, and it took only thirty to forty-five minutes to complete.

The effectiveness of the program was tested by administering it to 100 supervisors in one division of the company. This division had averaged several back injuries per month before the introduction of the program. Workers were given the usual training in proper lifting at the same time that the supervisors were given the program on behavioral conditioning. Back injuries as a result have been reduced significantly in the division where the system was put into effect.

DEVELOPING OBJECTIVES

The analytical part out of the way, our next task is to establish instructional objectives. Objectives fall into one of three broad categories: knowledge objectives, attitude objectives, or skill objectives.

Educational objectives dealing with changes of knowledge focus upon something students know at the end of the training period that they did not know at the beginning. This does not mean students know how to *apply* the knowledge. This objective merely states that students have the knowledge. We have to suppose that if the opportunity presented itself on the job, students would apply the new knowledge. If, for example, we are developing an educational program to teach the principles of effective delegation, an objective dealing with knowledge will read something like this: "What are the critical items in selecting the tasks to be delegated?" Given this question, 80 percent of the participants will be able to list all the items. If a student could answer that question at the end of the training process but could not answer it at the beginning of the process, we can assume that we have increased his or her knowledge during the process of the training.

The second category of objectives deals with attitude. Knowledge implies that something I know about has changed, whereas an attitude objective refers to my belief system. Coming into the training program, I had certain beliefs about management, people, supervision, motivation, communication, delegation, welding, or whatever subject area with which the training is concerned. A knowledge objective reads something like this: "Given a questionnaire with a statement, 'effective delegation can reduce firefighting by helping subordinates to anticipate problems,' the participant will agree." Notice that the objective does not suggest the participant knows anything more about delegation than he or she did before. We do know, however, that the participant thinks it is a good tool for reducing the amount of firefighting in an organization. From this change in attitude, we would have to conclude that if the participant had the knowledge and if the situation presented itself, he or she would practice the techniques of effective delegation on the job.

The third type of educational objective is the skill-oriented objective. An objective that focuses on skills or behavior reads something like this: "Given a job situation or role play in which the opportunity to delegate some tasks presents itself, the participant will select those tasks that are appropriate for delegation and apply the principles of effective delegation in passing the task on to a subordinate." Skill-oriented objectives are the best to work with wherever possible because they focus on the transfer of training to the job situation. They focus the energy of instructors, managers, and participants on the job situation, thus increasing the probability that the workshop content will be transfered back to the job.

Notice, however, that all three types of objectives—knowledge, attitude, and skills—are behavior-oriented. In the knowledge category, even though we are dealing with an internal criterion, we are seeking a behavior (answering the question correctly) that will indicate a knowledge change has taken place. Objectively dealing with an attitude, again, involves an internal change in somebody's belief, but we are seeking a behavioral reaction that indicates the change has taken place. The skill objective permits two ways of observing whether a particular skill has been developed: first, by watching to see whether delegation takes place in a role-playing situation; second, by observing changes in job behavior that indicate the skills have been developed and applied to the job situation.

Whichever of the three types of objectives is elected for the training process, some degree of behavioral change should be involved. Without behavioral implications to training objectives, we are left with only witchcraft, gut reactions, and warm feelings as a basis for determining the effectiveness and efficiency of the training as a behavior-change mechanism.

OBJECTIVE-ORIENTED CONTENT

The next step is to determine the content to be covered in order to meet the educational objectives we have outlined. Let's carry our delegation example further to provide continuity of thought in developing educational programs. For the knowledge objective, our list of subject matter content that should be covered looks like this:

I. Selecting Tasks to be Delegated
    A. Urgency vs. importance
    B. Effective use of your time
    C. Subordinate experience
    D. Accountability and authority

For the attitude objective, the subject matter content to be covered looks like this:

II. How Delegation Helps
    A. Problem anticipation
    B. Staff development
    C. As a training tool

And, for skill-oriented objectives, the subject matter contents look something like this:

III. Steps in Effective Delegation
    A. Identify tasks to be delegated
    B. Identify receiver
    C. Explain the task
    D. Check for understanding
    E. Follow up

Whereas this is not a complete course about effective delegation practices, let's presume that these are the only three objectives we have set for our workshop. We now have a topical outline that presents the subject matter content to be covered in order to meet our instructional objectives.

Thus far we have determined behavioral deficiencies on the job by subtracting the required behavior from those that the participants already possess. We then established our instructional objectives based upon those deficiencies and determined the specific content that needed to be covered to meet the objectives. Now we must select the most appropriate methodology.

TRAINING METHODS

Selecting the most appropriate method gives us a wide range of options. A variety of methods including both on- and off-the-job techniques are available to the individual wishing to change some-body else's behavior through training. Among on-the-job methods is job rotation. Under rotation, an individual moves from job to job usually at some planned interval spending perhaps three months each in sales, manufacturing, accounting, and the corporate office. Many organizations use this same method to help develop strength in the management team simply because an individual cannot rely on technical competence in moving from diverse areas of a business, such as from quality control to manufacturing to warehousing. One has to rely upon supervisory skills, which, by the way, get strengthened in the process.

Although job rotation provides a wide perspective of the organization as well as the functions necessary in operating different departments, one must rely largely upon the individuals within that department for the bulk of one's training. Employees on job rotation are probably not in the department long enough to refine their sense of that department. If they are interested in skills and in passing along that information, then their departmental experience in an area such as quality control will be fruitful; but if the individuals within that department are not skilled and just as inexperienced as the new employee, this job rotation will be a disappointment for all involved.

Coaching techniques are another popular on-the-job method. They are not unlike job rotation in that they provide experience within a department as a means of learning skills in that particular functional area. However, they differ from on-the-job rotation in that somebody is specifically assigned to do the coaching. Coaching usually occurs only in one department, often the department in which the individual is going to begin work with the organization. A common practice in this area is to have a new employee go out on calls with an experienced salesperson for a period of time until he or she "gets his feet on the floor." The disadvantage of both the coaching and job rotation techniques is that the individual being coached and trained may unwittingly pick up the ineffective practices of the person who is being used as a model.

A third possibility for "on the job" training is the use of task forces and special assignments. One organization, for example, undertook a company objective to reduce product costs by a significant amount. A task force consisting of representatives from marketing, manufacturing, quality control, production engineering, design engineering, and accounting was put together to examine the cost content problem and recommend specific solutions. The reason for putting the task force together in this manner was threefold: first, it provided inputs from all the areas that would be affected by such a cost reduction program; second, it provided for cross-fertilization between departments that carried implications far beyond those inherent in the cost reduction program. The individuals in marketing now were given a new view of manufacturing, engineering, and accounting. The accounting personnel presently on the task force knew where some other information systems broke down in terms of relevance, usefulness, and timeliness in relation to other departments. Throughout the company, there was a tremendous impact in terms of the cross-fertilization of what went on within other functional areas. Finally, the task force provided an opportunity for representatives from various departments to tackle problems that cut across functional lines and typically dealt with a higher level of the organization. Thus, in this case, the individuals on the task force were able to work on problems that were somewhat broader in scope than those they worked with in the past. This provided the opportunity for the vice president or department director in each area to pass along some information through coaching and counseling that otherwise would not have been passed along.

Off-the-job training methods also offer a variety of opportunities for selecting appropriate mediums. The most common mediums are (1) conference, (2) self-study, (3) correspondence study, (4) films, and (5) tapes and cassettes. Each of these has advantages and disadvantages. The most effective off-the-job training programs are a mix of these.

Conferences can involve lectures where the instructor talks to participants for a certain period of time. It can involve discussion in the form of small group conferences, panel discussions, or an open forum. It can involve case studies where participants in the workshop analyze a particular production process, quality control, or a marketing case, usually with teams that develop solutions to the problem. The most effective conferences seem to us a variety of role plays in passing along information. Role play allows for maximum transfer between the learning situation and the job situation, for it gives participants the opportunity in a relatively nonthreatening situation to apply the skills learned during the workshop. Trying these skills out and finding them not only useful but also relatively easy to use increases the probability that the workshop participant will apply these same skills on the job.

Self-study takes one of two general formats. "Programmed instruction" is a self-learning, self-paced design that calls for the participant to work through a series of teaching frames and make appropriate responses. After making the responses, the learner is able to match his or her response with the correct response, thus improving skills in a step-by-step process. Programmed instruction can be either off-the-shelf (for example, a programmed instruction manual on finance for the nonfinancial manager) or developed especially for a particular job situation, such as a company manual on how to repair a particular product. This can then be sent out to dealers, distributors, and owners of that product. An instructional manual is another form of self-study; although it closely resembles programmed instruction, it is usually not validated (i.e., tested to make sure it teaches exactly what it is supposed to teach) and usually does not call for responses on the part of the reader. It merely provides information and suggests specific steps.

Correspondence study is another method used in a variety of areas. It consists of a series of lessons in which the participant reads the information, studies the materials, and then completes a test or series of questions that are sent off to a central point for correction and feedback. A number of universities, for example, offer correspondence courses in principles of accounting. In these courses, which are usually developed and graded by faculty members, a student is assigned certain chapters and materials to read and then given a set of practice accounting problems. The student works through the accounting problems and then sends them to the university to be corrected. The method combines instructional manual and program instruction. The major differences are that correspondence courses are usually not as closely validated as program instruction and the feedback cycle is a little longer. However, they do provide more feedback than instructional manuals and are many times better designed. Additionally, many universities offer credit for a limited number of correspondence courses.

The final mediums are films, tapes and cassettes. Increasingly, a number of educational firms are offering films on motivation, communication, delegation, management by objectives, and a score of other management practices. Films and tapes and cassettes are also available in accounting, for instance, for the nonaccountant, drill press operation, and effective telephone operation. Some of these— how to be an effective telephone operator, for example—are designed specifically for a company for one particular job. Others (techniques of effective negotiating, for example) are used for all managers in a variety of situations. Moreover, an increasing number of firms that have sponsored public seminars and workshops are putting these same seminars on tape, combining them with the materials from the workshop, and packaging that workshop so that it can be done at home, in the car, or in a variety of geographical settings. Still others are providing instructional manuals for internal trainers and providing all the workshop materials and films necessary to make a workshop work.

None of these mediums, either on-the-job or off-the-job, is an end in itself. Each must be used in the proper location and at the proper time to maximize the behavior change that is sought. Indiscriminate use of any of these will often not produce any job behavior change and in some cases will even inhibit the desired behavior because of the adverse circumstances in which the program is offered. Someone seeking to maximize the behavior change on the job will find that there are a number of principles that can be put to work to increase training effectiveness no matter which medium is selected.

MAXIMIZING ROI IN HUMAN ASSET DEVELOPMENT

Capital investment in both human and nonhuman resources requires dollar outlays. Both kinds of investment can be used in a variety of ways to increase the probability of organizational success, and both have proven capable of doing just that in the past. Both types of investment will have to continue in the future if our economy is to continue to grow, and both will have to show and increasing rate of return on investment (ROI) if we are to utilize effectively all the resources at our disposal. The question is not, then, should we invest in capital or human assets. Rather, the question is, "How can we maximize our return from both investments?" The task facing the manager is not dealing with mutually exclusive events, but of maximizing the return from both of those events. With that thought in mind, let us examine several ways in which managers can maximize their return on investment in human resources.

Look for Job-Related Performance Change in Training Management

As it has elsewhere, the computer has made its impact in the field of management development. Role plays and case studies have proven invaluable aids in management development because they bridge that gap between knowing and doing. They offer participants the opportunity to practice application of skills, learn the consequences of that application, and receive realistic feedback without the possibility of unfavorable impact upon the organization.

Management games offer what is essentially a more sophisticated version of the case study. Computers store vast amounts of data and teams of participants are organized into mock companies, then they compete with one another under realistic conditions, with the computer providing rapid feedback on the quality of decisions made.

One major automotive firm, for example, conducts a week-long course for its dealers. An integral part of the course is a game that runs the entire week. Teams of participants are organized into dealerships and each team makes decisions during the class day. At the end of each day, their decisions are fed into the computer. The next morning the impact of their decision is reported to each team. Six months of business operations can be covered in one night. The result: an opportunity to practice in simulation actual job performance. There is usually a high degree of transferability of the program back to the job in using this method.

In another example, one company ran fifteen hundred managers through a speed reading course. The managers actually improved their reading speed and comprehension by 125.4 percent on the average. They now can read the sports page, novels, and the company house organ in a much shorter period of time than before the course. One observer noted that about one-third of the managers actually read more than twenty minutes per day on the job. He wondered why the other two-thirds were trained in that skill. Here we see a behavior change, but one that is not job-related.

Participants are generally considered to be at a management development program to change one of three things—knowledge, attitudes, or skills—the objectives we spoke of earlier. Although these may be worthwhile intermediate goals, attaining them is not enough; it is the application of these attitudes, skills, or knowledge that is important. They must be translated into new, different, or improved behavior on the part of the participant in the course—behavior that is related to job performance. Moreover, the behavior change must be related to the development effort—a sort of "before and after picture" that demonstrates that our manager has changed job behavior.

Check the Potential ROI Before You Develop

One of the most embarrassing questions a training director hears is, "Just what is management development producing for the company?" At the lower levels of the organization, the question can be answered with relative ease. People at that organizational level are processing goods and hardware. The results of training generally show up in some index that provides hard data for judging the effectiveness of the training. These indices include turnover, absenteeism, scrap loss, downtime on machines, units of production, retention rate of new hires, or skill level of machine operators. Information such as this is not only readily available but is usually closely watched. One or several of these indices can provide useful information on the results of training at lower organizational levels.

The person who looks for equally quantitative data higher in the organization, however, will be disappointed. As one moves up in the organization, the questions become more difficult to answer. The measurement and evaluation process involves results that are often intangible, that take longer to show up, and that are heavily larded with opinions, prejudice, and biases. Measurement is much more difficult where the environment supports mystical beliefs that learning, management, and leadership are philosophical and creative, thus placing them beyond the realm of mortal measurement and evaluation.

Between the two polarization points (how will this pay off in dollars tomorrow vs. training is imaginative and creative, thus immeasurable) lies the world with which the evaluation of management development takes place. That we need evaluation is inescapable. It provides the vital feedback loop that makes management development a system. If evaluation is to be effective, it would seem that an evaluation program should meet the following criteria:

1. Provide information to management as to the result of the training effort; that is, how close did the program come to achieving its established objectives.
2. Be administratively feasible; that is, practical to apply within the resources of the activity and with a minimum of expense and disturbance of personnel.
3. Provide for a systematic and unbiased means of collecting information.
4. Contribute information that can be used selectively to improve the training program.[2]

Without an evaluation and feedback system that meets the criteria described above, there is no way (except by chance) of making the adjustments along the way that are so often vital to the strength of a successful management development system.

Keeping in mind that we are working within an organization setting, we will not find it too difficult to pinpoint the four key sources of information that can be used for checking ROI decisions: (1) the superior, (2) the peer group, (3) the trainee, and (4) subordinates. Each of these sources—separately and in conjunction with one another—is effective within the scope of its biases and limitations. (Perceptions of changed behavior will change from source to source.) The indications of changed behavior are many and often complex. John R. Rizzo has suggested a few:

1. Changes in job performance of the participant. This includes actual management practices such as the application of human relations and work skills to the job situation; technical innovations; the number of profitable suggestions; percentage of management who perform well; and turnover and absenteeism.

2. Changes in the job performance of the participant's subordinates. This includes suggestions and innovations; productivity and improved performance; satisfaction and morale; turnover; absenteeism and grievances; and scrap records and downtime.

3. Changes in end-operational results. This includes policy changes; technological advances; personnel and production records; cost reductions; activity changes (more time spent in planning or coordinating); and structure changes such as new staff services.[3]

It seems reasonable to say that, at best, measuring ROI from management development is an inexact science. It is nevertheless one of the most important tasks that anyone responsible for management development efforts must take into account.

Make Sure the Job Environment Supports Developmental Efforts

Another essential step in maximizing ROI from management development is to decide whether the system will support the training that is given or planned. It is entirely possible that an individual might learn a behavior during training and be punished for that same behavior. When this happens the newly acquired behavior will fall by the wayside. One large wholesaler, for example, had carefully trained its inside salespeople (the individuals in the office who deal with customers that call in) in all the techniques of good salesmanship, including suggesting additional items, selling the full line, and pointing out special prices on certain items.

Yet, an examination of the accounts handled by the inside sales staff showed that the average yearly volume of each account seldom rose above $450 even at a time of heavy inflation. The individual to whom the sales staff reported had tried everything—coaching, counseling, pleading, yelling, and various combinations thereof. Nothing worked.

Then he looked at the consequences to the individual salesperson. When the account passed the $500 a year mark, it was considered large enough for an outside salesperson to handle, to whom it was turned over. Inside salespeople, however, worked on partial commission. Turning the account over to an outside salesperson caused the inside sales staff to lose its commission. Thus, to the inside salesperson consequences were negative for raising an account above $500 per year.

In another instance, a British manufacturer ran a course designed to improve supervisory effectiveness. The course was able to change supervisory attitudes, but the supervisors found that the new attitudes conflicted with management practices. This conflict brought serious organizational strife, disagreement, frustration, and even embitterment. Of the 97 supervisors who took the course, 19 left the company and another 25 sought other positions within it. Of those who had contact with top management, 80 percent became dissatisfied. In all, 83 of the 97 supervisors who took the course said it was a failure because it did not change top management attitudes. The dissatisfied group—those who either left the company or sought other employment—included nearly all the best qualified and most intelligent supervisors.

This principle is also readily apparent in the example of the subordinate who takes a management development course. The subordinate is taught about participative management and all the benefits that accrue when one allows subordinates to participate in decision making. This is fine, if the boss happens to be a participative manager. But many times we are teaching participative management to people who work for an autocratic boss. The first thing that happens when our newly developed manager returns to the job is that the boss corners the subordinate and says, "That may be fine for those professors, but that isn't the way we do things around here." Two weeks of training are reversed in one single sentence by the boss. Why? Just because the environment does not support the management development effort.

Without the approval of the superiors, the benefits of training may well be considerably less than when training receives support from the top. Moreover, in instances of active opposition to the training, the effort is dysfunctional.

Successful training involves not only acquisition but equally important is the maintenance of behavior. Too many management development efforts today direct themselves only to the process of acquiring behavior. Although they do an excellent job of enabling participants to become proficient in a skill they previously could not perform, management development efforts often fall far short of maintaining that same behavior on the job.

Even well-designed and carefully thought out training programs can fail because they are not supported on the job. Even the best of the training programs is of little use if the consequences on the job do not support the newly learned behavior. Indeed, many employee behaviors can be changed merely by systematically analyzing and rearranging consequences, as we shall see in the next chapter.

7
Identifying Consequences of Human Behavior

Results are the basis for measuring organizational success. Results come from individual performance, team performance, and organizational performance. The probability of well-trained employees producing good results is greater than the probability of poorly trained people producing good results. However, experience shows us that well-trained employees working toward a goal does not assure organizational success. Goal orientation heads things in the right direction and keeps the members of the organization looking to the future; but it does not ensure that the support will be there to keep the momentum going. Good results orientation is the spearhead of the attack; well-trained employees provide the troops. The day to day performance of individuals within the organization provides the momentum necessary to keep things moving in the right direction. If organizational results need to be improved, management must develop improvement programs that take into account individual

90

differences. Individual behavior provides the key to success once well-trained people are headed in the right direction.

Individual human behavior is an interesting and puzzling phenomenon that is at the heart of many productivity problems and successes. Machines and other capital equipment play a role, but the people who operate those machines and capital equipment make the difference between success and failure. Productivity is not a mechanical question but a people question involving the psychology of human behavior.

Let's examine job behavior of individuals in light of what behavioral psychology tells us about human performance. Why do people behave—for good or for bad—the way they do on the job? The answer is simply because it makes sense for them to behave that way. In working with thousands of executives in all kinds of job responsibilities—production, sales, manufacturing, quality control, warehousing, health care, government, and countless other organizations in both the private and public sectors—it has been my experience that people behave the way they do in organizations because it makes sense to them. This has led me to develop something that I call Connellan's Law of Human Behavior: *Every individual's behavior makes sense to that person.* What they do may not make sense to me, it may not make sense to you, it may not make sense to anyone else in the world, but it makes sense to that person in that situation at that particular time.

This is something that Dale Carson, a former FBI agent who accepted an appointment as sheriff of Duvall County, Florida, was able to recognize and make work for him. Carson noted that behavior problems with young toughs in jail were becoming increasingly serious. He analyzed the situation through the eyes of the misbehaving young toughs. For years, Carson's predecessors had put the young toughs on bread and water when they misbehaved in the prison. To us, that probably seems like punishment.

Carson, however, examined the situation not through his own eyes, but through the eyes of the young toughs. For them, he realized, the bread and water treatment was not punishment but reinforcement of tough behavior. Once released from prison, they could brag about how "tough" they had been in confinement. One can almost imagine their conversation.

"Hey, Harry, I see you're back on the street again."

"Yeh, they let me out, but I'm just as tough as I ever was."

"No kidding. How tough are you?"

"Hell, I'm so tough, they put me on bread and water, that's how tough I am."

It didn't take Sheriff Carson long to realize that the bread and water treatment was particularly reinforcing to the young toughs. The question he then faced was how to change their behavior. Puzzling over the situation, he hit upon the ingenious idea of substituting babyfood for bread and water. Young toughs who misbehave in the Duvall County Jail are no longer given bread and water. Now they receive strained beef, carrots, applesauce, and other baby foods. Sheriff Carson reports, "It's no fun to tell your buddies you were so tough they had to put you on baby food. A one-day diet of it usually gets them on their best behavior."

To put this in proper perspective, let's return to our earlier diagram of the ABC's of behavior. You may remember that we suggested that A stood for antecedent, B represented the behavior, and C the consequence of the behavior. The antecedent (that which precedes the behavior) tells us whether a behavior will occur the first time. The consequence (what happens after) tells us whether that behavior will ever occur again. In analyzing the job behavior of employees, we must look at the consequences to the individual of the behavior *as that individual perceives them*, not as I perceive them, not as you, their peers, colleagues, coworkers, friends, relatives, or neighbors perceive them. This basic law of human behavior underlies much of the technology upon which behavioral management is based. To the casual observer, to the boss, or to the personnel manager, the behavior of the subordinate may seem inexplicable, unreasonable, or even beyond belief, but to the individual, it is quite reasonable.

Keeping in mind that the consequences are only in the eyes of the beholder, we can develop two principles that will help us explain why the behavior does or does not take place:

1. If a behavior leads to positive consequences for the individual, the behavior will continue on the job.
2. If a behavior leads to negative consequences for the individual, that behavior will cease or diminish.

Simple in concept, the two basic principles of behavior become more complex in application. Karen Searles Brethower, a behavioral psychologist working in business and industry, and a pioneer in the field, has identified four corollaries useful in applying these principles to the job situation:

1. If one behavior is asked for, but a second behavior receives positive consequences, the second behavior will be the one exhibited on the job.

2. If a behavior leads to positive consequences for an individual under one set of conditions and negative consequences under another set, the behavior will be exhibited when it leads to positive consequences and will not be exhibited when it leads to negative consequences.

3. If a behavior is not called for on the job, or has no consequences, it will eventually cease.

4. The further in time a consequence is from a behavior, the less effect that consequence will have on the behavior.

The implications of these corollaries regarding behavior apply to the job situation. Let's consider the first corollary. A manufacturing firm I once worked with has spent a lot of money on human relations and on instituting democratic styles of leadership. Instigated and supported by the personnel director, the new style got off to a flying start. Everyone attended a week-long course on developing a democratic style of leadership. The personnel director and the company president had both written statements of policy that outlined the democratic approach to leadership and stated that this approach would be the company's policy for management practices.

Harry was one of the employees who took the course. He returned to his job full of good intentions to apply what he had learned in class. For three weeks he did pretty well. He talked over decisions with subordinates, sought their opinion on large and small matters, and tried including everyone in the discussions. He worked very hard at the democratic approach to leadership; in fact, he worked so diligently that some of his performance indicators began to slip slightly. Part of this was because his subordinates were unaccustomed to this new approach. For years, Harry had been the tough, hard-bitten, old-line foreman with a reputation for being gruff. The new, pleasant Harry was less gruff. Aware that his performance indicators were slipping, Harry worked all the harder at bringing things back into line. He talked things over more frequently with his subordinates and spent more time discussing alternatives and asking opinions.

By the end of the third week, a couple of the indicators were slipping seriously, and Harry began to show signs of the pressure he was under. By late morning on Friday of the third week, he couldn't take it anymore. He threatened to fire half his people, questioned the biological ancestry of the other half, and turned loose a barrage of invectives that would have made a drill instructor blush. Immediately, a complete turnaround occurred and things began to run like clockwork. They ran smoothly all afternoon and continued to run smoothly. Harry was complimented several times by the plant superintendent for taking strong leadership when it was needed. Harry never again engaged in, or even considered taking, a democratic approach to leadership.

Democratic leadership was called for, but Harry did not exhibit it. Instead, he exhibited the second behavior—a hard-line approach to leadership—which was reinforced when he used it not only by the plant manager but by the information Harry received about his job performance. All his performance indicators turned around and improved (a form of reinforcement), and his hard-line behavior was additionally reinforced by his boss.

In another instance, engineers were asked to submit monthly reports detailing the time and money that was involved in each project they worked on during the course of a month. These reports were to be used by the company management for product pricing and bid proposals. The behavior called for submitting accurate reports to management on a timely basis. In practice, however, this hardly ever happened. Reports were usually submitted late and were often full of inaccuracies. The behavior requested was seldom if ever exhibited.

If we examine the consequences of that behavior, it becomes apparent why the problem behavior occurred. When the engineers submitted their reports on time and they contained errors, the engineering staff manager returned the reports to the engineers for corrections. If, however, the reports were late and inaccurate, the engineering staff manager corrected them himself to save time rather than return them to the engineers for corrections. Again, the desired behavior was not exhibited because a second behavior—submitting the reports late with inaccurate information—was reinforced more to the engineers.[1]

The second corollary is clearly illustrated in the example of the child who has been taught that ice cream and candy are available only at certain times of the day and then only under certain conditions.

Michael is seven years old, and he knows he can have ice cream only in the middle of the afternoon or as a dessert. Neither ice cream nor candy can be eaten just before mealtime. For years, Michael's parents have been drilling this into his mind and now he behaves accordingly.

This summer, however, Michael turned seven and became eligible for his "big trip." All of Michael's brothers and sisters had made the trip each summer since they were seven, and this summer Michael's turn came to begin seeing the world. The big trip was a two-week vacation at Grandpa and Grandma's. Michael was dropped off by his parents late one Sunday afternoon for his two-week visit.

The next morning about 11:30, Michael and his Grandpa were at the drugstore to buy Grandpa some chewing tobacco. Michael noticed the drugstore's soda fountain and decided to test the situation. "Grandpa, could I have an ice cream cone?" Michael would never have asked this at home; he had learned that the answer is "no." Grandpa, however, is a pushover. "Why, sure, Michael, what flavor would you like?" Michael decides on a scoop of strawberry and a scoop of chocolate. Michael doesn't eat much lunch but does manage to stuff down three cookies that Grandma puts on his plate.

That evening Grandpa and Michael walked down to the drugstore again to buy the evening paper. Michael noticed a dazzling array of candy bars at the counter. He seized the initiative and boldly walked over and picked out a rather large-size chocolate bar that he put on the counter next to the paper that Grandpa was purchasing. Without blinking, Grandpa paid for both the paper and the candy bar. Michael learned quickly. Every day in the course of the next two weeks, he ate candy and ice cream at any time of the day he chose.

When he returned home, he tried the candy and ice cream routine on his parents. It didn't work and he was firmly rebuked. In the future, Michael has learned, he will ask for candy and ice cream during the two weeks he is at Grandpa and Grandma's. During the rest of the year, he will refrain from doing so because, although that behavior leads to positive consequences at Grandpa's, it leads to negative consequences at home.

In a more complex example, the army has had much the same problem as Michael, his parents, and his grandparents. During the late 1960s, training specialists in the army were engaged in converting several of the military occupational specialty courses to a self-instructional format. Programmed learning texts, self-instructional materials, and performance-based tests were designed by specialists. When the courses, materials, and tests had been designed, tested, redesigned, retested, and refined, they were tried on sample populations. Preliminary test results indicated that a potential savings of several million dollars a year existed for the army in the form of reduced training time, fewer instructors, and higher skills and performance levels on the part of the trainees. Excited by their preliminary findings, the specialists tried out the materials, courses, and tests at several training centers.

In several centers, the results bordered on disastrous. Although the first few groups of students who took the courses did as well as or better than expected, progress quickly bogged down. The students were taking longer and longer to complete the tests, and in some situations they took even longer than under the old system. Instead of saving time and money, it appeared as if the new self-instructional system might end up costing both time and money. Puzzled, the specialists checked to see what had gone wrong.

Here is what they found. The materials were working well. Most of the early students had finished in a shorter period of time than if they had used conventional instructional methods, and most of these had a higher test score in the performance tests. Some of the students had finished up to a week earlier; many had finished two to three days early. However, each of the students who finished early was put on some kind of detail. Some ended up on KP, others ended up on area beautification, and the balance were given other bothersome and unpleasant tasks to fill their extra hours. It didn't take long for word to get back through the ranks of the trainees that finishing the course early meant going on detail. The result was that more and more of the students worked slower and slower to ensure staying off detail.

After this information came to light, the training specialists persuaded the appropriate army officers to change the consequences of the students' behavior. Any trainee who finished one of the self-instructional courses early was given a three-day pass. No one finishing early was to be put on any detail.

The results were dramatic and immediate. The entire situation made an 180-degree turn; students were soon back on schedule, finishing well ahead of the time they might have taken had they been using conventional instructional methods. In the first situation, the trainees were punished for finishing early, so they ceased this behavior. In the second situation, the students met with positive consequences for finishing early, so they worked hard to finish early.

These same principles work in firms. One company with which I am familiar employed a very production-oriented general foreman and a housekeeping-oriented general manager. During most of the week, the plant looked like a pigsty. However, at 2:00 on Friday afternoon, the general manager always made an inspection tour through the plant. By 1:30 every Friday afternoon, the plant was shipshape. Right around 2:00, the housekeeping-oriented general manager made his inspection tour. By 2:20, conditions began to deteriorate, and by the middle of the next week, the plant once again resembled a pigsty.

Just as in the other situations, behaviors that led to positive consequences under one set of conditions were exhibited under that set of conditions; behaviors that led to negative consequences in a different situation were not forthcoming when that second situation existed.

The implications for the psychology of organizational success are fairly clear: if individuals are not performing correctly in one situation but they are in another, the consequences in that second situation lead them to perform in the desired manner. Changing job behavior is accomplished merely by rearranging the consequences so that they are positive in both situations.

Now consider the third corollary: *if behavior has no consequence, it will cease.* One firm I know with a rather large force of salespeople scattered across the country found it was losing control of its sales operation. One of its key problems was a lack of marketing information and customer data from the field. To remedy this problem, the company instituted a reporting system under which certain pieces of information were to be forwarded to the company on a weekly basis. With a relatively high degree of fanfare, as well as a short inspirational memo from the president, the system was put into effect. For almost a month and a half it worked well. Reports were mailed in on Friday; the majority of them were received in corporate headquarters in Monday's mail; and by Tuesday morning the corporate staff had compiled the information into a meaningful report that both marketing and production could use in preparing forecasts and making necessary adjustments.

By the sixth week of the program, however, the inevitable had occurred. A couple of salesmen forgot to submit their reports. Another remembered but didn't send it until Monday, which meant it was received at corporate headquarters on Thursday. In each of the three instances, nothing happened; there were no negative consequences. Moreover, there were no positive consequences for individuals who did submit their reports on time: these salespeople were never acknowledged, they never received the total compilation, and they never knew how corporate headquarters was using the information. Missing reports became more frequent and late reports became the norm rather than the exception. By the end of the third month, the information system was almost a shambles. Here's why:

1. Salespeople who sent in reports on time had no reinforcement for their behavior.
2. Salespeople who sent in reports late suffered no negative consequences or feedback for that behavior.
3. Salespeople who did not submit reports at all experienced no consequences for that behavior (or lack of behavior).

Although the behavior was called for and was said to be appropriate on the job, it was not reinforced when exhibited. The management system failed to discriminate between good behavior and bad behavior, so the sales force behaved accordingly. In their minds there was no distinction between sending in reports and not sending in reports or sending them in late. Although the company may have had some consequences in mind at the end of the year (bonuses, merit increases, promotions), it offered no consequences along the way.

One firm, for example, established a new suggestion program. It was introduced by industrial relations with support and endorsement from the company president. A form that was easy to use was designed and placed in strategic locations around the premises. Awards and prizes including a reserved parking place, a dinner for two, and a weekend for two were announced for employees whose suggestions saved the company in excess of a certain amount of money.

With a great deal of fanfare, the program began. Employees started looking for better ways of doing things. They kidded one another about who would win the dinner. Arguments developed about the best place to spend the weekend for two. In the first few weeks of the program, numerous suggestions were submitted.

However, by the end of the second month, the suggestions were down to a few a week. Employees who just a few weeks earlier had been enthusiastic participants in the program were now apathetic. By the end of the third month, the apathy had turned to resentment and people were openly complaining about the program.

All the prizes and awards were still ready to be awarded but there had been no feedback. Suggestions were not acknowledged. Employees whose suggestions were rejected received a form with seven boxes with the box indicating the reason for rejection checked (e.g., not cost-effective). Those whose suggestions were accepted were not informed of acceptance. At the end of the sixth month, the prizes were awarded and the program quietly disbanded.

In both instances—the sales reports and the suggestion program—job behavior had either no consequences or perhaps negative consequences, at least in the eyes of the performer. Brethower points out that if the behavior is not called for on the job or has no consequences, it eventually stops being exhibited. The task of the manager in these situations is to arrange consequences that favorably dispose the performer to behave in the desired manner. Often merely providing positive consequences (perhaps only a thank-you note penciled by the sales manager) produces a dramatic effect upon behavior.

Let us now consider the fourth and final corollary: *the effect of time on behavior.* Consequences removed in time from behavior have little effect on that behavior. The management process that most clearly demonstrates this corollary is the annual performance review. One manager has described this review as that time when the reviewer doesn't sleep the night before and the employee being reviewed doesn't sleep the night after. The wag's opinion notwithstanding, performance reviews are often very painful for both individuals. One of the reasons they can be so painful is that they are a cumulative summary of consequences (both positive and negative, but usually negative) for events that occurred over the course of a year. The pain comes not from the negative consequences (or even the positive consequences) but because this is the first time that feedback is received by the subordinate on job performance. Such reviews are often loaded with surprises, innuendos, and punishment for not achieving goals that might not have been previously established.

Most performance reviews as presently conducted do little to accomplish their central purpose: changed job behavior. Whereas short-term behavior change on the job may occur as a result of a performance review, that behavior seldom if ever lasts more than two or three months. Lasting behavior change cannot be accomplished by the use of performance reviews alone. Lasting behavior change is best accomplished by providing consequences at the time the behavior occurs, not months afterward. A simple encouragement, "That was a good report to the Executive Committee, John. You described what you were going to tell them, you presented the information in a fashion that was readily understood, you did it in a concise and brief yet complete manner, and handled the questions well," shortly after the report is given does more to change that employee's behavior than anything else separated in time from the performance. On the other hand, a simple, "Don't ever pad your expense account again," at the time the inappropriate behavior is discovered will produce a more lasting effect than ranting, raving, or pounding the desk that might take place at the time of the annual performance review. Small doses at the appropriate time have a more lasting effect than large doses separated in time. As time passes, the consequence has less and less effect on behavior. For this reason, performance reviews should be a cumulative summary of feedback about job results that has gone on during the course of the year. This summary should be used as a basis for establishing goals for a forthcoming budget period. The learning and behavior change takes place not at the goal setting time and not at the time of the performance review, but at the time of the feedback that takes place between those two times.

Providing positive consequences on an immediate basis has produced startling results for Emery Air Freight.[2] Emery is the nation's leading air freight forwarder; approximately half of its total costs go for transportation payments to the airlines. Emery is reputedly the world's largest user of D-size containers and pioneered the use of such containers. These containers reduce ground time for jet aircraft and cut handling costs for the airlines, thus earning discounts for Emery and saving on insurance by lowering pilferage and breakage costs. In checking system performance, Emery's dock workers were asked how they thought they were performing in relation to standard. The dock workers felt they were performing at about 90 percent effectiveness; that is, out of every 100 times they could use a container, they used one about 90 times. Their supervisor also thought they were doing about 90 percent, as did the operations manager, the station manager, the regional service manager, and the executive office operations representative.

Staff visits, however, showed that actual performance was at approximately 45 percent of standard, not 90 percent. This was not surprising performance when you consider that it takes extra time to load containers in the evening, when the biggest influx of shipments occur—coincidental with the heavy schedule of flight departures that allow little time for dock handling. Moreover, when a dock worker did load a conatiner, thereby saving the company money, nobody took the time to say, "We appreciate your taking the extra effort to load a container and help us save money."

Emery put into effect a simple solution. Each worker measured his own performance in relation to the number of containers used versus the number possible to use and passed that information along on a daily basis to his supervisor. For each improvement in performance or maintenance of improvement, however slight, the dock worker was praised by the supervisor. At all levels of the organization from the executive office down, each individual whose station or region showed improvement was given immediate reinforcement and feedback for that improvement.

Within one day, performance moved from 45 to 95 percent of standard. First-year savings from the program amounted to $650,000. Happily, that performance level has been sustained on a regular basis at the stations which continued the feedback and positive comments.

A tool and engineering company I know of was having problems with its phone bill. Phone charges were running 70 to 80 percent higher than charges for firms of similar size. Periodically, the president sent out a sharply worded memo reminding everyone that the phone bill was extremely high and recommending that everyone try to restrict his or her phone calls. This memo came out about once every ten months; yet seldom if ever was it distributed to everyone who used the phone. Unfortunately, aside from the memos, no one ever knew what the phone bill was. Although charges were received monthly, they were kept on a graph in the comptroller's office. The information was there, but it was not used to provide feedback for people whose telephone behavior affected the bill.

Two things were done. First, a statement of ways by which the phone bill could be cut was given to everyone who used the telephone (when to leave callback messages, when to call person-to-person or station-to-station, how to cut a five-minute call to a four-minute call, etc.). Secondly, a simple graph was designed and hung where everyone could see it without having to walk into the comptroller's office. Charges were graphed each month and any improvements were acknowledged. The phone bill dropped quickly by 23 percent.

What we are suggesting is that in any given job situation, individuals can perform in one of two manners. First, they can perform as desired on the job (filling out the job tickets, making calls, coming to work on time, producing error-free reports, etc.) or they can perform in an undesired manner (failing to submit call reports, coming to work late or not at all, packing crates improperly, welding improperly, etc.). Moreover, for either of those behaviors, one of two things can happen: something positive or something negative (see Figure 7.1).

Examining the consequences of job behavior is much like the work of a chemist or pharmacist, weighing the consequences of performance on a set of old-time scales. If performing in the desired manner leads to few positive and many negative consequences and performing in the undesired manner leads to many positive but few negative consequences, we will have a balance, as shown in the Fig-

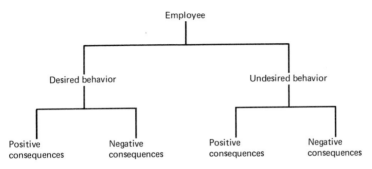

FIGURE 7.1   Consequence analysis

ure 7.2, and will not get the desired behavior. If, on the other hand, the desired behavior leads to many positive and few negative consequences, while the undesired behavior leads to few positive and at least some negative consequences, we will get the appropriate job performance, as shown by Figure 7.3.

This model suggests several things. First, we have to define very carefully the specific job behavior we want. It is not enough to deal with general abstractions such as motivation, commitment, interest, or good attitude. We must deal with specific behaviors such as submitting call reports, filling out job tickets, placing pieces in the right bin, using the customer's name, and getting the correct information from the patient.

The next step in the examination of consequences is to identify the consequences affecting each of those behaviors, to determine whether they are positive or negative consequences for the person performing the job, and then to place them in one of the following four categories:

1. Positive consequences for the right behavior.
2. Negative consequences for the right behavior.
3. Positive consequences for the wrong behavior.
4. Negative consequences for the wrong behavior.

With these four alternative methods of arranging consequences in mind, let's look at a personal example and see what might have been done to correct that particular situation.

I went to work many years ago on the production line of a large automotive plant. The last thing that occurred before I actually went on the job was my meeting with the safety director. I spent about ten minutes with him while he delivered a short lecture on the virtues and advantages of wearing safety glasses. He explained that burrs coming off the lathe could blind a worker or that oil flung off one of

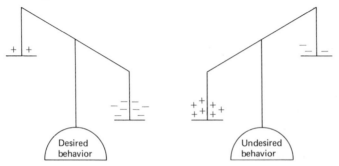

FIGURE 7.2   When consequences lead to undesired behavior

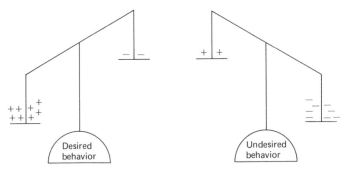

FIGURE 7.3   When consequences lead to desired behavior

the moving parts of the engine might permanently damage eyesight. I was given training on the correct method of wearing safety glasses, and I promptly put them on as I was quite impressed with the lecture.

The first day on the job I noticed that none of the other workers around me wore the safety glasses. None of them seemed overly concerned about possible damage to their eyesight, nor were any metal burrs flying off the equipment. Also, the glasses didn't fit correctly, and by the end of the first day my ears were sore where the glasses fit over them.

The second day I was still the only one wearing safety glasses, and my ears by this point were very sore, so I bent back the bow of the glasses so they wouldn't rub so uncomfortably. Then the glasses began to slide down the bridge of my nose, and I was constantly pushing them back up. My hands were greasy, and grease was soon all over my face and smeared on the lenses of the safety glasses. In addition, that afternoon several of my coworkers took me aside and asked whether I were trying to make them look bad by wearing the safety glasses.

Needless to say, the third day I didn't wear my safety glasses. I was asked to sit with the rest of the guys at lunch, they included me in jokes, and I was generally reinforced for not wearing my safety glasses. Had the safety director passed by my station on the production line, he might have concluded that his training was not thorough enough and hauled me back into his office to put me again through the safety glasses course. However, the problem was not truly one of training. I *could* perform the desired behavior correctly, but I was not doing so because the behavior of not wearing glasses was being reinforced on the job. .

Geary Rummler, president of Praxis Corporation, a Morristown, New Jersey, consulting firm that is a pioneer in behavioral engineering, calls this the "can do–will do" concept. The employee can do the tasks required but is not doing them because of the consequences that exist in the job situation.

The safety director or production manager might also have concluded that I was poorly motivated or had a bad attitude about the job. However, if my behavior had been examined in view of the consequences that happened in the job situation, it is not at all difficult to determine why I was not wearing my safety glasses. The question now becomes, how does someone get me to wear those safety glasses? Following the same basic model, it appears that the safety director has four options:

1. He can add positive consequences for the right behavior such as telling me he's glad to see me wearing safety glasses, making sure that I get the easier jobs, switching me from the 6-cylinder to the 8-cylinder line, switching me from afternoons to days, or countless other things that I would see as positive. The key thing to remember is that it is not the production manager seeing the consequences as positive that affects the behavior. It's whether I see that same consequence as positive.

2. He can remove negative consequences for the right behavior, like getting me another pair of glasses, refitting my glasses, refitting new glasses for me, giving me a pair of safety glasses to wear over my regular glasses, making sure all the people working around me are smaller than I, or any other one of a variety of actions that would remove the negative consequences for wearing safety glasses.

3. He can remove positive consequences for doing the wrong thing, such as separating me from my peer group at lunch.

4. He can add negative consequences for the wrong behavior, like warnings, layoffs, dismissal, verbal reprimands, written warnings, or anything else I would perceive as negative.

Of the four available alternatives, the fourth—adding negative consequences to the wrong behavior—is the one most quickly resorted to in many businesses simply because it is so easy to turn on the "lightning machine." The problem is, of course, that some days the lightning machine doesn't work or the operator of the machine (manager or supervisor) is not in a position to operate it. The addage "While the cat is away, the mouse will play" is a good example of the limited effect of giving negative consequences for the wrong behavior.

The easiest and fastest step with the longest lasting impact on human behavior is number one: adding positive consequences for exhibiting the right behavior.

To do this, we need an information and feedback system that tells us and the individual employee how things are going. Building such feedback systems is an important element in changing human behavior, and it is to that task we turn in the next chapter.

8

Designing Feedback Systems

To many people, feedback and reinforcement are the same thing. However, there are some important differences between the two that should be noted and clarified. There are reasons for treating the two separately.[1] One is that they come from different conceptual bases. Feedback and the notion of feedback derive from communications theory. Feedback is information (communications) about present or past performance that is communicated to the individual employee, presumably in a way that will influence future performance. Feedback gives employees information about their performance and can come from production records, quality control reports, sales records, annual budgets, computer printouts, or a variety of other sources.

Reinforcement, on the other hand, is a concept of the behavioral psychologists, who maintain that proper feedback (information about job performance) is reinforcing and that it strengthens job per-

formance, or increases the likelihood that the behavior being reinforced will occur again. Sometimes, however, the feedback does not
have the desired effect and is therefore not reinforcing. Thus, another
reason for treating the two separately is that feedback is primarily the
presentation of information to an employee about his or her job performance that may come from a variety of sources. It provides guidance and direction to the employee and is neutral in character. Reinforcement, however, focuses on how that information is used or can
be used to improve employee performance. Reinforcement involves
using otherwise neutral information to strengthen job behavior.

The third distinction between feedback and reinforcement is that
by examining them both, we can better interrelate two different areas
of interest to managers. One of these two areas is increased interest
and use of information systems in the area of data processing. For
today's manager, information systems play an increasingly important
role in making critical decisions necessary to run a business well.
Reporting systems are becoming more sophisticated; when asked
how things are going, today's vice president of manufacturing often
turns to a stack of computer printouts rather than telephoning the
shop. The second area of concern for today's manager is the development of human resources. Managers are finding that employees do
not automatically work hard and intelligently. It is no longer enough
to bring a person into the organization, describe the job, explain
what you expect, and ponder whether the new employee will perform
according to standard. If an organization is to perform, individuals
must perform. This requires skill development as well as skill maintenance for individual employees. By utilizing the increasing need for
and use of information with the concept of reinforcement from behavioral psychology, today's manager can make better use of information systems not only for decision making but also for improving
employee productivity.

A fourth reason for considering reinforcement and feedback
separately concerns the most fruitful areas for the application of each
concept. Applying the concept of feedback in analyzing and solving
human performance problems in a group, a department, or an entire
firm leads one to items otherwise overlooked in seeking solutions for
performance problems. Think back to our earlier illustration of the
welding department, the subassembly department, and final assembly to see how this notion might be useful. Specifically, seeking solutions to quality control problems within the welding department, if
we were to use only behavioral psychology approaches, we would
tend to look at individuals within that department and see what
factors might be reinforcing to that individual. Utilizing the notion of

feedback, however, we are helped by examining the welding department as a total performance system. We can view it not only as a performance system but also as a system whose outputs are fed into subassembly as input, and then we can see the relationship of those units to final assembly. Thus, using not only the concept of feedback from the welding department but also feedback from the two receiving systems (subassembly and final assembly), we can develop a technology for an improvement program that cuts across departmental lines.

However, if we look at the performance of one individual—who is tardy, produces poor quality work, or does not submit reports on time—the concept of reinforcement is more applicable. It aids us in identifying important items we might otherwise overlook. For example, we might be concerned with the habitual tardiness of one employee. Feedback systems as they relate to a department, work team, or entire firm probably aren't applicable in solving individual performance problems such as these. Reinforcement concepts from the area of behavioral psychology, however, can help us here to identify specific factors that will help reinforce the behavior we want from that individual and give us a basis for dealing with individual differences.

Having both concepts—feedback and reinforcement—aids us in directing our attention to important items in analyzing a particular performance problem. It also helps us build an all-inclusive performance improvement program that deals not only with individual performance but just as importantly with the performance of teams, departments, and firms. Moreover, utilizing both concepts gives us a basis for dealing with either systems or individuals and for identifying performance deficiencies in each.

In review, feedback is information delivered to the performer that controls performance. This information must be believable and provide guidance and direction to the employee in his or her performance and let the employee know how he or she measures up to job standards. Importantly, it provides a basis for learning and improvement.

In the absence of a good feedback system, employees eventually develop their own information system that compares them with some standard. Invariably, that information system is wrong and invariably their interpretation of the information is considerably more complex than what was intended in the original information system.

One firm I know of, for example, required its machine operators to keep the area clean around their machines. This entailed not only taking the scrap parts to a certain location on the production floor but also sweeping up the off-fall around the machine and keeping the area tidy. This was considered a standard procedure for the shop. For a while, the machine operators followed the program faithfully and the shop area always looked clean. Everyone picked up. However, as time went on, the final assembly department began needing more parts from the machine shop. Orders were increasing as the economy improved and line delays were becoming a problem in the assembly area. Eventually, the amount of work performed by the operators began to decline. The shop area became less neat but there was no information or feedback from the production manager, the superintendents, or the foreman. The machine operators then hardly cleaned up much at all. They had at this point changed their interpretation of the shop rules to give lower priority to clean-up than to production.

Finally, the shop became so messy that the production manager asked what had happened to the clean-up plan. This put feedback into the system but it occurred in a somewhat different manner than hoped. First, to get out some parts, the machine operators did not do a very thorough job. One, for example, hid some of the minor scrap parts in the offall underneath some boxes behind one of the machines. This event occurred about the middle of the afternoon one Friday just before the vice president of manufacturing came through the plant for inspection. The machine operators thus changed their interpretation of what was required. Feedback was telling them that the job requirements meant to keep the production floor clean—not the entire shop area—when an inspection of the plant was to be made (i.e., not all the time). In conversation with these individuals some time after the fact, it was clear that they had no guilty conscience about this occasional and haphazard clean-up program. Each felt that he was using his time in accordance with the real needs of the firm. As a group, they believed they were fully occupied in producing parts and thus had little time left for clean-up work around their machines. Whether their interpretation of priorities was correct (in this case it was not because of some of the unique properties of the steps of the operation), what is important is that their interpretation of what was required of them had changed because of the feedback they were receiving.

Feedback, of course, as pointed out by the preceding example, does not always work. Karen Brethower has identified six situations in which feedback will not work. It's been my experience that each of these six situations occurs frequently. The first is that if the feedback is used as a basis for punishment, it will not work. This use of feedback often leads to such behavior as falsification of records. In this situation, the information and feedback system is used in a punitive fashion rather than as a basis for self-control by the employee. This condition is usually accompanied by a lot of arm waving and desk pounding as the manager looks at the report and finds that the error rate is running at 5.5 percent. In a loud voice while pounding the desk, he makes his feelings known by saying, "I see from this report that the error rate is running at 5.5 percent. If I have told you once, I've told you a hundred times; We cannot tolerate an error rate above 3 percent. I don't want to ever catch you with an error rate of above 3 percent again. Now get out of my office and get back to work."

This stern admonition when accompanied by the arm waving is usually successful. The supervisor won't *catch* the employee with an error rate above 3 percent. The error rate might be above 3 percent, but the supervisor won't "catch" the employee. When the information in the feedback system is used for punishment and fault finding, employees very quickly learn that it is best not to report all the information (in this case the error rate) because the boss really gets upset when that happens.

A similar situation exists when the feedback is about variable A but payoff is associated with variable B. Specifically, management says it wants behavior A, insists on behavior A, and probably even sets goals on behavior A. However, it often happens that when we look at the payoffs within the organization—either financial or social—we find that employees are being paid off on behavior B, not on behavior A. This causes short-term confusion among employees but not for long. They quickly figure out where the payoffs are and conclude, probably rightfully, that this is the behavior the organization wants. Often the employee interprets the conflict between what management says it wants and the likely payoffs as a case of management's saying it wants one thing, meaning it really wants another, with payoff provided for a third behavior.

This was illustrated for me several years ago as I walked through the main plant of a midwestern manufacturing company. In preparation for an upcoming project for that organization, I had been talking with the vice president of personnel to get a sense of the human environment within the plant and with the executive vice president to get a feel for the direction the company was taking. Both had communicated to me an intense desire and interest in assuring equal employment opportunities for all minorities. Since this was before the big push for compulsory compliance on the part of individual firms, I was rather pleased by the stand that both of them had taken.

They admitted they felt the firm had unintentionally discriminated racially in the past, and they were committed to hiring more members of minorities for their work force.

The third step in my orientation was with the production manager of the main plant. His task was to give me an operational view of the activities within one of the company's typical plants. As we walked through the plant, he pointed out the various operations, describing the processes used in manufacturing their product line, and in general orienting me to the company's production methods, as well as specifying some of the performance problems within the organization. About two-thirds of the way through the plant tour, it suddenly occurred to me that there was some incongruity between what I had heard in the front offices and what I was seeing in the plant. Although I had not asked, it had been emphatically stated by both the vice president and the director of personnel that the hiring of minorities was an important part of each manager's job. Yet as I walked through the plant, I was struck by the fact that most employees were white males. The fact that the plant was filled with white males and the front office was saying that they had a campaign to hire minority-group employees seemed in conflict. I questioned the production manager about this apparent discrepancy.

"Oh," came the response, "I can see where that would be confusing. It's true the front office tells us that one of the things we have to do is hire minorities. However, it has been my experience that it takes a lot longer to train these minorities than it does to train people who have worked somewhere else and have job experience. That extra training time cuts down on production levels and sometimes keeps us from meeting our shipping schedule. I have seen people fired around here for not meeting production schedules, but I have never seen anybody fired for not meeting an EEOC (Equal Employment Opportunity Commission) goal. They send me reports every month on how we are doing in meeting the EEOC goal, but I don't pay much attention to them. What they are really interested in is meeting the production schedule, and that is what I pay attention to. They say they want us to hire EEOC people, but I think what they mean is they want us to hire minorities if it doesn't interfere with the production schedule. However, hiring minorities usually interferes with the production schedule, so what I am going to do is concentrate on meeting the production schedule and worry about hiring minorities at some other time."

Unreasonable behavior? Perhaps from your point of view or from my point of view, but to the production manager, it is perfectly reasonable. The company said they wanted behavior A when they meant they wanted something else, but the payoff was an entirely different direction.

A third situation in which feedback won't work is when it is too late. While managers today are suffering from information overload, part of that overload is simply that the information they receive arrives too late for them to take any corrective action. One firm with whom I worked, for example, had a quality control report that came out on the 16th of the month. This meant that employees receiving the report were receiving feedback on something that occurred somewhere between two and six weeks earlier. Not only is it impossible to take corrective action by that time, it is extremely difficult even to remember the variables that were affecting quality then. Although employees of this firm read the report to see how they had performed the previous month, they could do little to correct whatever was responsible for excessive scrap rework or rejects. The feedback system utilized in this case was of little or no use. It provided an interesting historical perspective on the company's accomplishments during the previous month, but it certainly was not of much use to managers who needed information to make decisions and take corrective action on a daily or weekly basis.

Receiving information two weeks after the close of the month is somewhat analogous to asking athletes to wait for two weeks to find out how they performed. You can't do it and expect results. One of the reasons that some football players, for example, perform well on the field is that they are guided by a series of good feedback systems. One such system, of course, is the yardline markers on the field. As the runner progresses up the field, he has something that tells him how he is doing literally each step of the way. The yard markers don't clap and cheer but they do present information to the performer on his progress toward the job goal. The concept is easily transferred to the business situation. One of the interesting things is that when reinforcement of the behavioral psychology is combined with feedback from information systems, the feedback itself can become reinforcing. The football player, for example, has listened to the claps and cheers of the crowd as he passed the yardline markers on the field. At some point in his career, probably fairly early, the yardline markers served not only as a feedback mechanism but also part of a system that provides for self-reinforcement and self-control.

A fourth area where feedback is not effective occurs when the performer is not in control of what needs to be changed. Many organizations have good feedback systems that rapidly provide specific information on job performance for employees. However, that information concerns a performance variable over which the employee has no control. Information of this sort is of little or no use and often hampers job performance by its adverse effect on the outlook of employees subjected to that job information.

For instance, one firm with whom I worked was concerned about line defects in its final assembly operation. "Line defects" in their language consisted of defects in the final product as it rolled off the end of the assembly line and went through final inspection. Some of these line defects were very clearly due to errors in the final assembly area. Others, in fact the majority, were not under the control of the supervisor or the employees in the final assembly area. Some of the line delays were caused by part shortages either from machine shop, welding, or subassembly. If a product rolled off the end of the line without a necessary sprocket, that was considered a line defect and the feedback information system fed that back to the final assembly area. It made no difference why the sprocket was not on the machine. The cause could have come from a variety of sources including a miscalculation by inventory control, a breakdown in the production scheduling system, a failure on the part of materials handling to move to the proper location, or any other countless reasons. But the feedback didn't occur until final assembly.

In an effort to control the defects from the final assembly area, a graph was hung there listing the average number of line defects per machine produced. Instead of having the intended effect of reducing defects, other things happened. One week the department worked particularly hard to control line defects and felt they had done an exceptionally good job. When the number of line defects per machine for that week was posted, the employees found that instead of going down, defects had increased. At this point workers became extremely discouraged and statements were heard such as, "Why try harder, it doesn't seem to make any difference? We are getting blamed for someone else's mistakes; how can we tell whether what we are doing pays in improved quality?" And for good reason. The number of line defects per machine had indeed gone up that week, but the increase was due entirely to problems generated by other departments, namely subassembly and production scheduling.

When the defects generated by the final assembly department were sorted out from the rest, it was discovered there was a significant drop in that number. Shortly thereafter, two lines were posted on the graph: total number of line defects and line defects generated by other departments. The receiving system thus had its own feedback system. It became clear which line defects were generated by final assembly and which defects were due to errors in other departments, which now could also get information on how they were affecting the final output of the firm.

The fifth area where feedback problems occur is measurement of and feedback on the wrong variable. This is best explained in terms of the four areas in which performance was measured earlier: quantity, quality, timeliness, and cost. Most jobs are affected by all these variables, but often feedback systems are set up to measure only one indicator. The most common occurrence is where quantity of output is measured and information regarding quantity is fed back to the individual employee but no measurement or feedback takes place regarding quality. When the feedback system is measured in only one of two variables, the employee tends to focus efforts only in that area of the job. This leads to out-of-balance performance by the employee. Where the feedback system, for example, in manufacturing is unidimensional rather than multidimensional, employees become highly concerned with production but not at all concerned with quality, time, or cost considerations. When the feedback system in accounting is unidimensional in accuracy, you tend to get extremely accurate reports that cost too much to generate and take forever to produce.

Again, feedback that is unidimensional rather than multidimensional leads to employee performance that is out of balance. The cure for this is worse than the disease, particularly when the feedback system as described above is used as a basis for punishment. Consider, for example, in case of a manufacturing operation where information regarding quantity of production is fed back to everyone but no information regarding quality is fed back. Let us presume, and it is a natural presumption to make, that the net effect of this is that the firm's production rate is very high but its quality rate is very low. At some point, these quality problems will come to somebody's attention, and if that person happens to be the arm waver and desk pounder, the manager comes down hard on those responsible for production. "You guys are turning out a lot of junk. I want you to tighten up and keep our production at a high-quality level. We are known for our high-quality products, and by God, you guys better shove high quality products out the back door." Very quickly, the behavior of the employees changes as they are unsure of exactly what the trade-off is between the two. They now conclude that quality has become much more important than quantity and behave accordingly. They are now getting information feedback on quality, and because of the behavior of the production manager that goes along with that information, they have concluded (perhaps rightfully so) that the company is not so concerned with production as with quality. Gears shift and suddenly the firm has a total reject scrap and rework rate of less than one-half of 1 percent of the direct labor hours. Unfortunately, production has been cut by 26 percent so the schedule starts slipping. Back comes the hammer about production. The net effect of this is a seesaw effect, tipping first on the side of quality, then on the side of quantity, never really balancing the two, or working to get both up at the same time.

A sixth area in which feedback systems don't work is when they require too much effort to record the feedback. Here again, sports provide an interesting analogy. It is not too difficult to record the total yardage gained by the halfback, divide that by the number of times he carries the ball, and come up with an average of yards per carry as useful information and feedback to the employee, the coach, and the general manager. This is information that is available, in the system, and easy to record. Consider, however, how scorekeeping and statistics would change if we wanted to change that to the average number of steps per carry. Someone would first have to count how many steps each person took in carrying the ball. This would be an extremely difficult piece of information of which to keep track. Do you count whole steps or half steps also? Does a step forward count the same as a step backward? How about a step sideward? Moreover, it would be extremely difficult to see all the steps a football player takes, particularly the last four or five steps when a swarm of tacklers is around him and it's hard to tell whether he is taking one step or four. All that is clear is that he went forward another half yard.

Much the same situation exists on the job. It is frequently too costly or too time-consuming to count and record the information that would be most useful for affecting human performance. On the other hand, sometimes just an inexpensive 3-by-5 card carried by the employee can provide the basis for a good feedback system. In instances of this type, it is often useful to have outside control as well on the feedback systems so that you feel confident that what is recorded on the 3-by-5 card is what is actually taking place.

FEEDBACK SHOULD BE SPECIFIC IN RELATION TO A GOAL

Specific feedback gives the employee precise information on his or her progress in relationship to a goal and avoids the problems of generalizations that do not provide precise information. Feedback to the employee who lacks a goal is information given with no purpose. Without a goal in mind or some target, employees do not know whether they are performing well or poorly. It is difficult for them to define the below-standard performance areas of their job. It also leaves the manager without information on individual or team performance. Feedback without a goal is like yard markers on a football field without a goal line or goal post: we can use these markers to measure how many yards we covered, but we can't tell whether we are moving in the right direction, nor can we tell when we have reached the goal line.

Combining feedback with goal-setting has proven to be a very effective technique for many organizations. In one firm, for example, the president determined that return on investment could be improved significantly if the firm were able to reduce substantially its inventory levels. Although the inventory levels were in line with production levels and sales levels were consistent with what they had been over the past five or six years, the president met with the vice president of operations to see what might be done. They agreed upon an objective to reduce the inventory levels from 5 million to 3.5 million over the following six-month period. To reach this objective, different parts of the firm undertook appropriate steps that would lead to the reduced inventory levels. Manufacturing, for example, undertook a commitment to reduce the inventory of work in process without affecting the production schedule. The objective "to reduce inventory levels of work in process from $750,000 to $500,000 by June 1, 1977, without affecting the production schedule" was posted; a large graph was also posted in several prominent places in the production area that ran from zero dollars to $1 million up the left-hand side and from January through June across the bottom. Each month progress was plotted as the inventory level inched downward. By June, the company had not only met but exceeded its goal.

Purchasing, on the other hand, undertook an objective that read: "to decrease the amount of lead time that purchases are landed on the docks of the plant from an average of four weeks to an average of three weeks before the scheduled need for the part in production." This objective was posted at a prominent location in the purchasing area, and over the objective was a graph laid out over a 26-week period. The graph indicated the dollar value of parts that were landed on the dock in the receiving area of that plant less than three weeks before production line time. Each week, receiving tallied up the dollar value of the parts received that week and noted when they were received, then fed that information back to the purchasing department. Purchasing began working out the details of the new plan with suppliers, and within two months, 50 percent of the materials were landing within the three-week deadline; within four months, 85 percent of the materials were landing within the three-week deadline; and at the end of six months, 90 percent of the materials were landing within the three-week deadline. The entire program was a success; the company exceeded its inventory level objective and dramatically improved its return on investment.

The vice president of operations credits part of the success of the goal accomplishment to just the fact that the goals were stated specifically and that each part of the organization had sub-objectives leading to the overall objective. However, he stated that the real credit must go to the people who worked long and hard on making that part of the program a success. He says they were motivated, they were dedicated, and they did the job. Much of the reason for their involvement and commitment to the success of the project he attributes to the fact that the feedback was not only immediate (monthly and in some cases, weekly), but more importantly, that it was posted in a prominent location where all who were working toward that particular objective could see it.

The vice president reported further, "Manufacturing, for example, was working very hard to make sure that units needing repairs, additional parts, or other items were moved through the production area quickly, thus reducing the work in process inventory. At the end of the month, they could look up at the graph and see that what they did during the previous four weeks had impact on the work in process inventory." The same thing holds true for purchasing. Someone might spend several hours working out a revision of a release order with vendor, and within two or three weeks, he could see on the chart how his specific activities two or three weeks previously were already having an impact in making progress toward the company's objectives.

A distributor-wholesaler likewise found that combining feedback with goal setting proved beneficial. The head of the accounting department in this particular firm was having some performance problems with one individual. This employee was averaging sixteen errors per week on invoices. Other than generalized exhortations to improve accuracy and an occasional chewing out, no firm commitments had been made by the employee to improve job performance. Sitting down with this individual, the department head had at length obtained a commitment to reduce the error rate to an average of five a week within 90 days. Each week, the individual was to record the number of invoices returned due to errors in manufacturer's code, product code, or customer code and chart the data on a graph. Within two months, errors were down to an average of five a week and were maintained at that level.

It is not enough, however, to make the feedback in relation to a goal. Feedback must be related to the proper goal. One firm, for example, installed a goal-setting program with a heavy emphasis upon sales goals. Over the following 12 months, they met all their objectives. In fact, sales were the highest they had ever been in the history of the firm. Unfortunately, profits were down. An analysis of why sales were up and profits down highlights the importance of selecting the right target. In this particular firm, as in many others, items with the biggest dollar value (i.e., those that would contribute most to the dollar volume sales objectives) were not always those with the highest gross margin dollars; in many instances, they were items that had the lowest gross margin dollars. Moreover, items that had the lowest gross margin dollars were often the easiest to sell because they were, in fact, priced so low. When this conflict between volume and profitability was pointed out to management, they quickly changed the objectives of the sales area from dollar volume to contribution dollar objectives. Within a short time, sales had leveled off and some product lines even dropped a bit, but profits were up substantially.

Thus, if a feedback system is to be effective, targets or goals should be built into the system. Many feedback reports (although fortunately, fewer and fewer) do not contain a target or goal so that managers can determine, for example, how far scrap, absenteeism, or advertising dollars are off target. Not only should goals be built into the reporting; they should also be built into the feedback system that provides information for employees who need that information for making operating decisions and taking corrective action.

WHEREVER POSSIBLE, FEEDBACK SHOULD BE SELF-ADMINISTERED

This provides immediate data for the employee on his or her performance on a weekly, daily, or sometimes even hourly basis. Employees who measure their own performance are more likely to accept information regarding it from an outside source and are thus more apt to respond positively to their job problems and to take corrective action. This is particularly true of new employees. New employees must first be able to evaluate their own job performance before they can get up to speed on their job. New employees should not be thrown in over their heads and allowed to sink or swim; rather, they should be put in a situation where it is difficult to swim, but as they build strength from the job, they continue their improvement. Good feedback provides information and the basis for learning so that the employee can more quickly learn when he or she is doing well and more quickly become independent of close supervision.

It has been my experience that when employees measure their own performance, they quickly become their own supervisor. This provides more job satisfaction to employees because they can now supervise their own efforts. They no longer require that somebody stand over them all the time telling them what to do.

EXPRESS FEEDBACK POSITIVELY INSTEAD OF NEGATIVELY

This avoids the development of employee attitude problems that are often caused by supervisors who criticize continually or who are always talking about negative aspects of job performance.

For example, one firm with whom I work on some performance improvement techniques was having problems with their chief mechanic. The vice president of the company took me aside one day and confided in me, "Tom, I wish you could give me some coaching and counseling techniques for dealing with Mike. I can't seem to get along with him and can't seem to get through to him anymore. All we are doing is fighting whenever we sit down and talk about the job." "Well, what causes you to fight?" was my response. "What do you talk about with him?" "What the hell else do you talk to a mechanic about? We talk about downtime on the equipment. It's his job to keep the equipment running, and if we have a lot of downtime, we are losing dollars because people are standing around waiting for the equipment to be repaired." Upon probing further, I learned that the equipment was down about 13 percent of the time and everytime this individual sat down with the head mechanic to talk about it, the head mechanic became defensive and came up with a long list of possible reasons why the downtime was running at 13 percent. The problem, it turned out, was not a coaching problem, a counseling problem, an attitude problem, a management skill problem, or even a mechanical problem. It was a feedback system problem. I suggested that whereas the equipment was in fact down 13 percent of the time, it was up 87 percent of the time. The feedback system needed to be changed from the measurement of downtime to the measurement of uptime. Instead of sitting down and talking to the mechanic about why the equipment was down 13 percent of the time, the manager should now talk about how to get the equipment from 87 percent to 92 percent. Stress the positive, not the negative. The uptime of equipment in this particular case is presently averaging 95 to 96 percent, and the only change in the job situation was the change in the feedback system from a negative to a positive measure.

FEEDBACK SHOULD BE IMMEDIATE

In fact, the sooner, the better. With immediate feedback, the employee knows of his or her present performance in relation to a standard. As soon as performance starts to fall below that standard or even moves in that direction, it becomes quickly apparent and the appropriate solutions can be developed, usually by employees themselves. More time is then spent on fire prevention or taking corrective action before the error rate moves from 3.8 to 4.1 percent, rather than taking fire fighting action or correcting the error rate after it passes the 5 percent mark.

Consider, for example, the problem with suggestion systems. Many managers spend a great deal of time discussing the importance of suggestions with supervisors and employees. Posters are put up on the bulletin boards claiming "We want your ideas." Announcements are made in the company communication mechanism or house organ that stress that ideas are welcome from all employees. Posters reading "Dream vacations to be given away" or "Employees earn money for saving the company money" are placed in prominent locations. Yet the ideas still do not come rolling in. Why not? Often because of a lack of immediacy and feedback.

What usually happens is something like this. An employee submits an idea to the suggestion department and to the supervisor and then waits and waits. Finally, about four months later, he asks whatever happened to his idea. He is informed that the committee that reviews suggestions is overloaded with suggestions right now and have not had the opportunity to review his suggestion yet. "However," he is told, "I am sure that they will probably get to it pretty soon now." It has been my experience that at this point, the employee quickly makes a mental note not to bother to submit any more suggestions. He reasons, "They say suggestions are important; they put up all these damn posters that tell us ideas are needed, then when I submit one, they don't even have the decency to let me know that they have received it. Not a thank you, not a note, not even a rejection, nothing. I wouldn't even mind being told 'no' if they told me quickly."

In working with firms on suggestion programs, it has been my experience that two feedback systems are needed. One provides immediate information that does no more than acknowledge receipt of the idea and indicate when the employee might expect further information or a decision on his idea. Later, a second feedback system tells the employee whether the idea is accepted or rejected. The immediacy of the first feedback, the acknowledgment of the receipt of the idea, has a much greater effect on the rate of suggestions than whether or not the idea is ultimately accepted or rejected.

In designing effective feedback systems, it is important to send the information to the individual performing the job, not to anyone else. The person performing the job is responsible for maintaining job standards. Feedback helps the individual meet standards. Too, the feedback identifies performance areas that are below standard so that the employee can improve performance accordingly. I have found that much information generated in firms goes to the wrong person or is used inappropriately.

Consider the case of the marketing department manager of one firm who has a budget report that tells him what percentage of the advertising budget has been expanded to date by month and by category. It's a very detailed and presumably useful report. Unfortunately, the manager who receives the report is one level below the head of the advertising department, who decides what to spend, where to spend it, and when to spend it. The decision maker is thus receiving indirect feedback at best on his expenditures to date. This is an example of the feedback system sending information back to the lower levels in the organization.

Out of every 100 problems with the feedback not going to the person performing the job, only 10 percent of them are this type of problem. The other 90 percent are cases where the information goes to too high a level in the organization. Scrap, rework, yield, and reject information often go to a plant manager and eventually filter down to the people who need it—the foreman and operators. It has been our experience in designing feedback systems that affect human behavior and performance that more information than necessary goes to a higher level of the organization. Too much information goes to top management and stays there. Too much information goes to accounting and stays there. Too much information goes to finance and stays there. Too much information goes somewhere and stays there. It does not get built into a feedback system so that it gets to the people who can use that information and let feedback guide their job performance.

RELEVANT FEEDBACK SHOULD GO TO
ALL LEVELS OF THE COMPANY

The key word in this assertion is "relevant." Relevant information is that which tells an individual about his or her performance. Unfortunately, much of the information used for feedback is irrelevant, at least to the situation at hand. If information is relevant, then management can recognize specific performance problems and allocate the necessary resources to help solve those problems. If there is a problem with market penetration and the advertising budget, then the appropriate level of the organization can allocate resources if it receives the proper feedback. If there is a problem with scrap or rework, then the quality control manager should receive the relevant feedback so he or she can allocate resources to help solve that problem. If relevant feedback goes to the appropriate level in the company, any manager can recognize employees' progress and use that feedback as a basis for reinforcement, thus ensuring that improvement will continue to take place.

Finally, feedback should be graphically represented. People tend to think in pictures. Employees may not "understand" a series of numbers but they do understand the graphs where lines move up and down.

The use of graphs has a much more substantial impact on employee behavior than merely feeding back raw data or numbers. Using a good graph can help give the employee both details about the situation as well as the big picture. Employees can look at a graph and see that rejects have fallen from 2.6 to 2.4 percent and associate that decline with some direct behavior on their part on the job. Employees can also look at the graph, and see that the reject rate has been coming down over the last six months. The psychological impact of this on individuals is great because they can look at the graph and see that what they are doing on the job in fact has impact upon organizational results. When employees' individual efforts are combined with the feedback system, they know the results of their efforts. Both the efforts and the improved performance are reinforced by the feedback system described in the next chapter. When this occurs, it has been our experience that the performance will continue to improve.

9

Reinforcement Techniques: How to Develop Behavior

Joe shook his head. Sure was a funny place to work, not a bad place but different. Ever since they asked him to monitor his own work and record on a chart next to his machine the units he produced and his average hourly yield, things changed. First of all, he figured that some kind of speed-up was coming. That's the way it is in most shops. To prepare for the worst, he started to build a buffer. He was a union member and figured that the worst that could happen was a lot of yelling by his foreman. He let his production slide and dutifully recorded it on the chart and waited for his foreman to come by. He did. Joe waited for the yelling and screaming about the drop in production. In fact, he spent three hours the night before thinking up excuses.

Mike, his foreman, looked at the chart, smiled, and thanked Joe for keeping the chart up to date and accurate, turned on his heels, and left.

Joe didn't know what to do. This had never happened before. Maybe Mike didn't realize that production had dropped. Joe made a mental note to remind him.

The next day Joe held production steady at the new and lower level, and when Mike came by, he pointed out the drop. Mike said he had noticed it, but more importantly, he noticed today that production had held steady without dropping further and thanked Joe for whatever it was Joe was doing to stop the slide.

Stop the slide? Joe had caused the slide; in fact, he could do any damn thing he wanted to. He sure couldn't figure Mike out. Most other foremen Joe had worked for yelled at the least little thing that went wrong and Mike had thanked him for stopping a slide in production. Mike might be a little crazy, Joe decided, but he wasn't all bad.

It had been three weeks since the new system was installed, and Joe noticed that his production was up 7 or 8 percent since the graph was started. What is more, yield was also up. Joe had stopped fiddling with his output after the first week or week and a half. There was no point in it. It wasn't any fun. Mike never got excited. The closest Mike ever came to being excited was the day output turned up a little. Mind you, it hadn't turned up by much, only from 50 to 52 units per hour, but Mike sure noticed it. In fact, Joe could almost remember word for word Mike's response when the graph turned up. Joe had been standing by his machine, straightening things up a bit before the shift ended. Mike had come by and picked up his graph as he usually did once or twice during the day. As he picked up the graph, Mike turned to Joe and said, "Joe, I see production has gone up from 50 to 52 and your average percentage of good parts has gone from 96 to 96.2 percent. Whatever you are doing to improve both of these seems to be really working; we're making good progress in the right direction and I appreciate the extra effort that has gone into that progress. If there is anything that I can do to help you keep that movement going, please let me know."

Joe remembers well his response to this. Caught somewhat off balance by Mike's remarks, Joe had said, "Thanks, I try to do a good job." Mike had turned to Joe again and said, "You sure do, and not only do you try, but whatever you are trying seems to be working and working well. We are definitely making progress in the right direction." Out of words now, Joe had smiled, mumbled thanks, and turned back to cleaning up his work area.

It was then he began to think. Mike was a different kind of guy to work for, that was for sure. First of all, he didn't put pressure on you like other foremen had in the past. Of course, Mike was interested in production, no question about that. He was always coming around and looking at that graph trying to figure out how to keep up production. Moreover, you never knew when he was going to come by and look at it. Sometimes he came by four or five times in one day. Another day he might come by only once or twice. Some days, he didn't even come by at all. You never knew for sure when he was going to come look at the graph. Why, one day Joe remembered that Mike had looked at it four times in the morning and only once in the afternoon. Then the next day, he came by only once. The day after that, he didn't come by in the morning but came by twice in the afternoon. Then the next day, he came by twice in the afternoon.

That was different from a lot of other foremen. Most foremen had a set schedule and you could count on their coming by at a certain time, say, between 10:00 and 10:30 in the morning or 3:00 and 3:30 in the afternoon. You never knew when Mike was going to come by, but Joe had figured out pretty much what Mike would say by now. If both graphs were moving up (units produced and average hourly yield), Mike would compliment Joe on the movement. If both graphs were moving down, Mike would not say anything except thank Joe for keeping an accurate graph. He'd say that accuracy was important to provide information in order to make decisions and to take corrective action on production problems. The only time Mike had spoken sharply to Joe was when neither one of the lines fell below the dotted line marked "standard" on the chart. Once or twice, the production or the yield had fallen below this line, and although he didn't yell and scream, Mike did say to Joe that, as they had discussed when they put up the graphs, anything below the dotted line was unacceptable performance. He had then asked Joe what steps could be taken to get the production yield back up above the minimum acceptance level. That, too, was different from most foremen. Most foremen always asked Joe why the problem was occurring, as if looking for someone to bully. Mike wasn't interested in bullying anybody; he just wanted to find out what kind of things might work in the future. Every idea Joe came up with that seemed remotely workable Mike was interested in trying.

If the graphs went in different directions, if, for example, production went up and percentage yield went down, Mike complimented Joe on getting his production up and then asked how they could get yield up to where it was. There was no question in Joe's mind that Mike was extremely interested in production. It was just that he went about it in a different way than most supervisors.

Mike was practicing the techniques of positive reinforcement. The "Mike and Joe" scenario is being repeated in all types of organizations—sales, manufacturing, quality control, health care—with good results. Mike wasn't practicing his reinforcement techniques in a haphazard fashion. He was, as we will see later, deliberately using positive reinforcement, extinction, and a variable schedule of reinforcement—three of the most powerful tools in changing employee behavior. What is unique about Mike's approach is that he applied these techniques in almost the reverse manner of the way you and I typically apply them in our business and private lives. Most of us, inadvertently perhaps, reinforce undesired behavior on the part of not only our staff and employees but also our family. The child, for example, goes outside and tramples through the flowers, and what happens? He gets Mom and Dad's attention. To be sure, there is probably a lot of commotion, but he also gets a lot of attention in the process, which is probably what he is after. If he goes inside and reads a book, Mom or Dad figures, "Gee, that's really terrific," and then go downstairs to finish gluing a chair back together. Dad and Mom ignore the kids when they read, ignore them when they tie their own shoes, ignore them when they use their fork and spoon correctly, but the minute they do something wrong, the children get attention in a variety of ways.

The same thing happens with the sales personnel. We ignore them when they turn in their daily reports, when they make calls, when they get new accounts, when they do all these things, because we figure that's what they are being paid for. When they get our attention, however, is when they don't do some of those things. We are usually inadvertently reinforcing the wrong behavior and extinguishing or getting rid of the behavior that we want.

"Wait a minute," you say. "Sounds as if you're putting the cart before the horse. People should do a good job because that's what I'm paying them to do. I pay employees to do a good job and, therefore, they should get their attitudes in shape and do a good job." Frequently, this statement ignores facts at hand. The people to whom we are usually referring when we make that statement are already doing a poor job and getting paid. Therefore, whether you or I like it or not, they are being paid for doing poor work. Since the person is already being paid for poor performance, there is, economically speaking, little incentive to perform well. While we might consider changing future economic relationships (i.e., suggesting that the individual seek employment elsewhere), for the present we are paying for poor performance.

TYPES OF REINFORCERS

Identifying or predicting what you will use to reinforce behavior for specific individuals is a difficult task. There is no magic formula for that selection, as only the person being reinforced determines what reinforcers will work for her or him. In no other domain of human behavior is the old bromide more true: "What's sauce for the goose may not be sauce for the gander." The only sure way to identify what reinforces an individual is to try something that you think might be a reinforcer and see whether it works. If the behavior you are trying to reinforce increases, then the reinforcer you have selected is a good one. If the behavior does not move in the direction you want, then it is not doing the job and you should select something else.

Ideally, the reinforcer selected should be immediately available, reusable, and under your control. Immediacy is, as we have seen earlier, one of the most important principles in using feedback systems and/or reinforcers effectively. Reinforcers separated in time from an action you want to reinforce have less impact than those that are used immediately. Although the concept of immediacy may not seem to be that important, it does help explain, for instance, why people miss work on Friday or Monday (immediate) even though they know their pay will be considerably less a week or a week and a half later (delayed). It also helps explain why giving someone this Friday afternoon off to play golf or go shopping is many times more powerful as a reinforcer than giving a two-day all-expenses-paid weekend in a resort six months from now.

A reusable reinforcer has much greater value than one that can be used only once or twice. Some of the reinforcers listed in Table 9.1, for example, are reusable time and time again. These include such diverse reinforcers as naturally occurring reinforcers, opportunities for growth and freedom, and social reinforcements (the most important kind). Other items used as reinforcers are not particularly reusable even though they might be used as many as three times. These include fringe benefits, promotions, and environmental changes.

Some reinforcers that might be effective are not under control of the manager who would like to use them. Take the case of the manager who wants to give someone a title as a means of reinforcement but can't. Dispensing titles may not be under his control. He might want to give someone assistance but this, too, may not be possible or under his control. It has been our observation that in selecting reinforcers using the three criteria of being immediately available, reusable, and under the reinforcers' control, the reinforcers that seem to

TABLE 9.1   Examples of Reinforcers

Reinforcer	Example
1. Control over job	Flexible time, choice in overtime, early start on vacations, schedule own work.
2. Job content	More responsibility, task force participation, represent department at meetings, participation in decision making, opportunity to learn a new skill.
3. Job environment	Air conditioning, new paint, less noise.
4. Money	Bonuses, fringe benefits commissions, merit increases.
5. Naturally occurring	Satisfaction of a job well done, sense of accomplishment, seeing the results of one's work.
6. Social	Recognition of a job well done, praise, award pins.
7. Status	Name on door, personalized company stationery.

be most useful are freedom, time off, social reinforcement, growth, and power.

Probably the most powerful reinforcers and yet the most often overlooked are social reinforcers. Finding something to compliment an employee about may seem like a trivial thing, but recognition seems to satisfy a universal need. In a recent survey, thousands of workers in the United States were asked to list factors contributing to their job satisfaction. Appreciation of work performed came in first. Unfortunately, its practice is not always in first place. You and I as practicing managers too often neglect to express our appreciation to the individual employee. The employee in turn concludes, "They don't care, they never say anything." It is, of course, not enough just to say "Nice job" to someone. For maximum effect, the reinforcement should be specific. For example, if an employee turns in a report, it's not enough to say "Good job" because she doesn't know what that means. What was "good" about it? She needs to know that. It's not even enough to say "This is a good report" because the compliment still doesn't tell why the report is good. If we fail to specify what is good, the employee may even conclude the report is good because it was typed on erasable bond. The fact may be that the report is good because it is concise, well written, and to the point. Show her. Be specific. If we point out one section that is exceptionally well done (i.e., because it ties the specifics into the big picture), point that out too. Using positive reinforcement does not constitute a continual series of "attaboys." Use of positive reinforcement suggests that very specific reinforcement be used so that employees are not only reinforced but know specifically why what they are doing is commendable.

If you can't determine some reinforcers to use in your own work situation, there are two possible ways to select or refine reinforcers other than consulting Table 9.1. One, curiously enough, is simply to ask directly what the employee would like, a technique used by a young manager at one of the major automobile manufacturers. After having been put in charge of a line that assembled rear-end units for trucks and buses, he discovered that although the standard was 72 units an hour, workers were lucky if they completed 45 units. Being fairly new with the company, the young manager asked the people working that particular line what it would take for them to bring their output up to standard. After talking it over, they decided that if they were permitted to get in an extra smoke break once in a while, that would justify an increased effort on their part. The final deal was that once they had completed 72 units within a given hour, the rest of that hour was theirs for a smoke break. It took only about a week before the workers produced up to standard within 35 minutes; they took the remaining 25 minutes for their smoke break.

Both the manager and the workers were aware that the situation could not continue indefinitely, so they renegotiated the agreement. This time the standard was raised to 92 units per hour, which they were able to produce and still get a ten-minute smoke break. Everything was fine until one of the divisional vice presidents, hearing of the improved production, came down to see what was going on. As luck would have it, he showed up in the middle of a break and raised the roof; increased production notwithstanding, those workers were being paid to work eight hours a day, and that was exactly what they were going to do.

Needless to say, the employees went back to "working" eight hours a day, and production went back to below the original standard. The new supervisor's unorthodox reward was visible and accessible, and there was no doubt that it was effective. The real question revolved around the choice of having a labor force that produces or one that merely puts in time.

The second option for finding an appropriate reinforcer is to watch the behavior of the person you are trying to reinforce and identify the reinforcements he or she is responding to now. For example, you might go down the list of reinforcers in Table 9.1 and select a reinforcement (bonuses, fringe benefits, promotions), then try to think of other examples in that category that this individual is working for right now. Select some specific examples in the second column for which the individual is working and use them as thought starters to come up with other types of reinforcers.

You might also listen to that person in a conversation during a coffee break or lunch or while he or she is not actively engaged in work. What are some of the things the individual likes and dislikes? Does the conversation give you a clue as to what the individual does either on or off the job during a few moments of spare time? During coffee break, for instance, the individual may talk a great deal about duck hunting, describing in detail the methods of placing a decoy, types of ducks, limits for each, and so on. This could be something to tuck away in the back of your mind; then, if that individual does a particularly good job, sometime in early fall you might reinforce his commendable behavior by saying, "Bill, that was really an exceptionally well-done report for these reasons." Be sure to identify the reasons. "I really appreciate your taking the extra time over the weekend to get it in. When the opening day of duck season comes along and if you would like, why don't you take the day off and see if you can get some."

Another possibility is to watch what types of things the individual does first when he or she is allowed to schedule his or her own work. If you can identify them, this is a good opportunity to apply the Premack Principle. The Premack Principle is named for David Premack, who noted that behaviors that occur more often can be used to reinforce behaviors that occur less often. This is the principle used by most parents (probably without realizing the scientific behavioral principle behind it) when they say, "You can't have any ice cream until you finish your spinach." The principle also suggests that if one behavior occurs more frequently than another, the more frequent behavior can reinforce the less frequently occurring behavior. If, for example, I play tennis more often than I mow the grass, playing tennis can be used as a reinforcer for mowing the grass. The statement "As soon as you finish mowing the grass, let's go play some tennis" makes sense in this instance. The game of tennis thus becomes a reinforcer for mowing the grass.

Whatever reinforcer is selected, it must be consistent with an individual's self-image. Anything that enhances the self-image serves as a reinforcer, and anything that threatens that self-image is resisted. If an individual perceives himself as well organized, then whatever reinforces that self-image will serve as reinforcers. Conversely, that same individual will not be reinforced by things that threaten the self-image. A person's self-image may also be quite different from the way others perceive her or the way she actually is. An employee may see herself as very efficient and hard-working (her self-image), while she may be poorly organized and make very ineffi-cient use of her time. Using the principles of reinforcement, we must build on that perception and use it perhaps even to move that indi-vidual from inefficient to efficient use of time. "Ellen, I noticed that list you are making up each morning of things to get done during the day seems to help office organization improve even more." This would enhance Ellen's self-image of being well organized (even though she may not yet be well organized). It also increases the probability of her continuing to use the list. If she continues to make up the list each morning, the probability of her becoming better organized increases. We then end up with a well-organized employee who uses time efficiently, rather than a poorly organized employee who does not use time efficiently.

CONTINGENCY MANAGEMENT

An important part of behavioral technology is the use of contingen-cies for reinforcers. This implies an "if-then" relationship (i.e., if behavior "a" occurs, then reinforcer "b" will follow; if behavior "a" does not occur, then reinforcer "b" will not be given). The important thing to remember in using contingencies is the "if-then" relation-ship, for this relationship if often reversed. The way it works is some-thing like this: "If you mow the lawn, then you can play tennis. If you practice the piano, then you can play baseball. If your work is com-pleted, then you can leave early on Friday afternoon. If you turn in your travel voucher on time, then you will be paid this month."

The way most managers get in trouble with contingency man-agement is by reversing the process. They make it a "then-if" process and the statements go something like this: "You can play tennis if you will mow the lawn afterwards; you can go outside and play baseball if you practice the piano afterward; I will give you Friday afternoon off if you will catch up on your work Monday morning; I will rush it through so you get paid this month if you turn your future ones in on time." The problem, of course, is that the process is reversed. If the contingency management situation is reversed to "then-if" from "if-then," the "if" seldom, if ever, comes to fruition. The proposition is interpreted more like, "I will go and play tennis but I may or may not get the lawn done. I'll go and play baseball, but I may or may not complete all my practicing. I will get Friday afternoon off, but it might take me more than Monday morning to get caught up. I will let you rush my expense voucher through this time so I will get paid this month, but I may or may not turn it in on time in the future."

Contingency management can also be used to teach response discrimination. Occasionally, it is desirable to obtain a behavior in Situation A and to eliminate that same behavior in Situation B. If the individual is reinforced in Situation A but not in Situation B, he or she is more likely to exhibit the behavior in the first situation than in the second. When this occurs, discrimination behavior has been developed. It is possible then to teach specific antecedent-behavior relationships.

Another good example of contingency management is a technique that has become increasingly popular in organizations today—participative management. Failure to use contingency management in relation to participative management, according to Frank Petrock, a behavioral psychologist from Ann Arbor, Michigan, is how most participative management systems have broken down. Petrock says that the participation is never made contingent upon anything. Just as the smart mother knows that permission to go to the basketball game on Friday night should be made contingent upon mowing the grass before the game, a smart manager knows that participating in decision making should be made contingent upon good work performance. Thus, one of the consequences of good performance is increased freedom for participation in decision making. Most participative management systems have not built in this contingency. Participation is there whether or not good performance exists. Thus, people who perform well get to participate in decision making, and people who perform poorly likewise get to participate.

If participative management is to work well, it must be made contingent upon good performance. People, departments, plants, and divisions who perform well should have more opportunity for freedom in decision making and should be allowed to participate in the decisions that affect their lives within the organization. If they are unable to perform properly, however, then permission to participate should be reduced or withdrawn. This does not mean that a good performance must precede participative decision making, but rather that continuing participation should be contingent upon improved performance.

Thus, a plant might be producing at a minimum acceptable level. The plant manager might well say, "You have an opportunity to shape the variables that affect your everyday lives here on the job. You have the opportunity to make changes and decisions, small ones at first and larger ones later on as the program proves successful." However, the purpose of this change in decision making is to improve performance, profitability, and productivity. As long as performance continues to improve, the department head's freedom in making decisions will continue to increase. If, however, performance does not improve, then the situation requires that the manager step in and take back the reins once again until some system is figured out that once allows an increase in the amount of participation in decision making. Thus, continued participation is contingent upon continued good performance.

In one of the two situations below, the salesman is reinforced for wearing a particular type of jacket and in the other he is not.

Antecedent	Behavior	Consequence
Sales call on new client	Wears loud jacket	No reinforcement
Company party	Wears loud jacket	Reinforcement

The key thing in helping the salesman make this distinction is to make sure the reinforcement is contingent upon wearing the appropriate attire at the appropriate time. If the reinforcement is not contingent upon the appropriate attire for the situation, then response discrimination will not occur; that is, he will not know when to wear a loud sports jacket. This then leads to the situation described earlier where we say we desire one kind of behavior but the payoff (in this case, social reinforcement) leads the individual in another direction. If no reinforcement were to occur in either situation (wearing the loud sports jacket appropriately or inappropriately), then the salesman would not be able to distinguish between the two situations. He would quite naturally conclude that it did not make much difference which jacket he wore because he had no feedback to the contrary.

The result of this situation usually occurs when we begin to hear the phrase, "But I told him a hundred times not to do it." The problem is that we may indeed have told him a hundred times and that (the antecedent to the behavior) is enough to start the behavior occurring. However, unless the consequence (in this case, the social reinforcement or compliment) follows the behavior, the behavior is not likely to be continued.

SHAPING

Shaping is one of the least understood, least used, but most powerful tools in behavioral technology as applied to the job situation. Its power in terms of changing job behavior is way out of proportion to its simplicity. Human beings are complex behavioral systems, and substantial changes in such complex systems do not occur overnight. They can occur rapidly and we can help them occur more rapidly than they might otherwise occur, but in no case do they occur overnight. The application of shaping is based on a common sense observation of human performance: people are not consistent in their performance. Job performance varies, being sometimes better, sometimes worse. To use shaping to its maximum potential, it is important to reinforce changes in performance that are in the right direction.

Let's take the case of a wholesaler-distributor who has an employee on the inside sales desk averaging six line items per order. The general manager feels that an average of ten line items per order is solid performance. At the end of a three-day skill-building workshop the manager had an action plan outline to improve the job results of this particular employee. A specific part of that plan was reinforcement for each step in the right direction. The manager explained the target of ten line items per order to the employee. The employee agreed to the target. At the end of the first week, the employee's average number of line items per order was 6.7. The typical manager's response at this point might have been one of the following:

1. To ignore that and grumble about the employee who wasn't "motivated" or "dedicated."

2. To chew out the inside salesman for not meeting the agreed upon target.

Neither of these courses of action was followed. Instead, the manager reinforced the employee—not for hitting 6.7, but more importantly, for *moving* from 6.0 to 6.7. What was being reinforced then was not the 6.7 but the movement in that direction. The statement that was used when this happened was: "Jim, I see that we have gone from an average of 6 line items per order to an average of 6.7 line items per order. It seems as if the new techniques we discussed are working because we are making good progress in the right direction. Is there anything else I can do to help you keep up the progress toward our target of 10?"

Clearly, the employee receives specific information on job performance and gets reinforcement for doing specific things on the job. Had the general manager said, "Jim, I see you have hit 6.7. That's really great," performance would no doubt have leveled off at that point and the employee would have concluded, and rightly so, given the wording of the reinforcement, that although the manager said 10 was the target, 6.7 was really acceptable.

The reinforcement techniques worked. Within five weeks, the inside salesman was averaging 11 line items per order and has been averaging that or very close to it ever since.

Shaping requires that we are able to break down a job into smaller steps and set up a systematic way of providing a reinforcement for a success within each of those small steps. All of us like to succeed. Success in and of itself is reinforcing to us. Shaping involves structuring a job so that the employee is succeeding most of the time. The tasks required of each employee should be difficult enough so that they involve some stretch and some learning, but at the same time, these tasks should not be so difficult that it is impossible to succeed or that the probability of success is very low.

It is an important skill to learn how to pinpoint the particular degree of difficulty where the tasks required of the employee are small enough for him or her to be successful and to learn the task, yet difficult enough to involve some learning and stretch. Determining that point depends, of course, upon the employee's familiarity with the situation, the type of skill required, the experience in the area, the relationship with the employee, the employee's relationships with peers and colleagues, and a variety of other job factors. There is no formula that tells you what that point is and how to reach it. However, one measure is clear. If a person begins to fail on a task, you may be expecting too much too soon. It is often wise to allow a drop to a somewhat lower level of performance. Once the individual is succeeding at the lower level of performance, then you may begin to require more of him or her.

Shaping is much like the tale of the man who lifted a calf the day it was born and lifted it every day thereafter until it was full-grown. It is virtually impossible for a man to walk into a field and lift a full-grown cow. However, it is at least theoretically possible that one could do this by lifting the calf each day, thus "shaping" one's ability. In much the same manner, it is highly unlikely the inside salesman can increase his performance from an average of 6 to 11 line items per order in one or two weeks, although improvement of that magnitude in that time has occurred. It is much more likely that you will be able to increase performance, but over a one-or two-month period. The probability of going from 6 to 7, and then 7 to 8, 8 to 9, 9 to 10, and finally to 11 is much greater than the probability of going from 6 to 11. Shaping requires noticing and reinforcing each of these improvements, thus increasing the probability that the improvement will continue.

Shaping can also reinforce some initial behaviors on the part of the employee that lead to the increase in the number of line items per order. We might, for example, notice the inside salesman suggesting added items to a customer on the phone or mentioning some product lines on which we had specials, or thanking a customer for calling our firm first, which gives us a greater chance of filling more of the orders. Each of these is a specific behavior that leads to the job result of increasing the number of line items per order. Early in the program, such as when the employee is moving from 6 to 6.7, 6.7 to 7.5, it is also wise to reinforce some of the initial behaviors both at the time they occur and then again when discussing results with the individual employee.

"Harry, I noticed you suggested additional items to ACME Construction. I know that takes a little extra time on the phone but I appreciate it and it is the type of thing we need to help us continue moving toward our target of ten line items per order." This is a statement that could be made at the time we heard Harry talking on the telephone. Then when we discuss with Harry at the end of the week how we are progressing toward our target, we can say, "Harry, I see we have gone from an average of 6 to 6.7 line items per order. Your strategy of suggesting additional items as well as mentioning on the phone the product lines that we have on special this month seems to be working. Keep up the good work, we're moving in the right direction. If there is anything else that I can help you do to get to our target of ten, please let me know."

SCHEDULING REINFORCEMENT

Constructive utilization of reinforcement techniques depends not only upon what type of reinforcer you use and upon the shaping principle; it also depends on when the reinforcer is presented and how often it is used. Thus, to utilize effectively these reinforcement techniques, it is necessary to understand when to use which schedule of reinforcement. A reinforcement schedule is nothing more than a plan for the presentation of reinforcement. Table 9.2 gives a variety of options for scheduling reinforcement. One option, of course, is to use no reinforcement at all. At the other end of that range of choices is what behavioral psychologists call "continuous" reinforcement. Between these two extremes are a variety of different combinations, permutations, and mixtures. Common sense leads us to conclude that continuous reinforcement is most effective because it is at the far end of our range. After all, we might reason, a person no doubt would work harder for a "sure thing." Not so. Intermittently scheduled reinforcement usually elicits a higher performance level than a continuous schedule of reinforcement. There are times to use both but over the long haul, the intermittent schedule obtains much higher levels of performance from an employee than a continuous reinforcement schedule. Here's why and when to use each.

Continuous reinforcement is reinforcement presented after each correct behavior on the part of the employee. This leads to a high rate of performance as long as the reinforcement continues to follow each response. An employee used to continuous reinforcement very quickly loses that behavior pattern when the reinforcement is withheld.

Vending machines provide a good example of this. They usually reinforce you by giving you candy, foods, soft drinks, cigarettes, and so on each time you use them. But suppose that downstairs from where you are reading this is a candy machine. Mary is used to stopping by the candy machine each day after lunch and buying a candy bar. You decide to watch Mary and see what happens. Every day she walks by the machine, drops in a dime, and gets a candy bar. This has been going on for three months now. Mary is on a continuous reinforcement schedule. This morning, however, Mary walked by the candy machine, dropped in a dime, and nothing happened. She pounded the top of the machine a few times and kicked it once or twice, pushed the coin return button, hit the machine a few more times, swore to herself, and went to the candy machine on the next floor to buy candy. After about ten seconds she gave up even though she was previously reinforced every time she used the machine. In fact, it is precisely because she was reinforced each time that she gave up so quickly when the reinforcement stopped. If Mary goes by the same candy machine tomorrow and gets the same treatment, she will probably never use it again even though next week it may be fixed. Why? Because she had been on a continuous reinforcement schedule that stopped and she has now "learned" that this machine doesn't work because it keeps money and gives no candy. Actually, two behaviors were extinguished or eliminated in this example: (1) putting money into the machine and (2) pounding on it.

Let's look, however, at what would have happened had Mary been put on an intermittent rather than a continuous reinforcement schedule. A good example of intermittent reinforcement scheduling is found in the type of vending machine generally found in Las Vegas. (In fact, the behavior developed from using intermittent reinforcement schedules is many times termed "slot machine behavior.") People in Las Vegas stand in front of a machine and put money into it

TABLE 9.2 Types of Reinforcement Schedules

Reinforcement Schedule	Designation and Description	Example*	Effect
No reinforcement		No response to productive behavior.	Reduces or eliminates productive behavior.
Continuous reinforcement		Employee reinforced each day production hits 100.	Maintains or increases productive behavior. This schedule is especially effective when used at the beginning of a behavior-change program. As long as the reinforcement continues, the behavior continues. However, the reinforced behavior quickly terminates when the reinforcement stops. Such a high frequency of reinforcement may lead to satiation. Continuous reinforcement is particularly appropriate for new, unstable, or low-frequency behaviors.
Ratio: reinforcement: (1) fixed ratio	(FR–4) A fixed number of responses must occur before reinforcement occurs.	Employee reinforced after every fourth day that production hits 100.	Productive behavior occurs at a high rate. This is usually a pause in behavior after reinforcement. Employee would probably take it easy for several days immediately following reinforcement. This schedule produces a high rate of response that is vigorous and steady.

Schedule	Description	Example	Effect on Behavior
(2) Variable ratio	(VR–4) A varying or random number of responses must occur before reinforcement occurs.	Employee reinforced on average every fourth day production hits 100. Sometimes this would be on the third day and sometimes on the fifth day.	No pause after the reinforcement. This schedule produces a large amount of work for a minimal amount of reinforcement producing a very high rate of behavior that is vigorous and resistant to extinction.
Interval reinforcement: (1) Fixed interval	(FI–(4)) The first response after a specific period of time as elapsed is reinforced.	Employee is reinforced the first day production hits 100, after four days have passed.	Productive behavior increases in frequency as the time for reinforcement approaches. Behavior resulting from this schedule is rather unstable, causing peaks and valleys in performance. The valleys immediately follow reinforcement and the peaks immediately precede reinforcement.
(2) Variable interval	(VI–(4)) The first response after varying or random periods of time have elapsed is reinforced.	Reinforcement becomes available the first day production hits 100 after an *average* of four days have passed. Sometimes three days would elapse and sometimes five or six days might elpase.	Generates great persistance in productive behavior even though reinforcement is long delayed. This also (like the variable ratio) produces a high rate of behavior that is vigorous and resistant to extinction.

Source: The information in this chart was adapted in part from Fred Luthens and Robert Kreitner, Organizational Behavior Modification Glenview, Ill.: Scott Foresman) 1975, p. 51.

* Technically speaking, the examples used are slightly incorrect. A very strict definition of *response* would be in terms of one production unit. However, for practical purposes in the organizational setting, we have defined a response as 100 units a day.

all day long, even though they get reinforced by hitting the jackpot only occasionally. Moreover, the specific intermittent reinforcement schedule they are on is variable ratio. The machine pays off on the average of once every 20 times. However, it may pay off the first time, the 20th time, the 21st time, the 36th time, the 60th time, the 62nd, the 63rd, and the 64th time, and then not again until the 101st time. The player knows the machine will pay off but is never sure when. It is this gamble that keeps the behavior at its high rate.

When a behavior is being learned, of course, we can move from a continuous reinforcement schedule to one where behavior is reinforced only once every 20 times. Reinforcement must be done gradually. First once every two times; then once every three times; once every five times; and once every ten times, and so on. Interestingly enough, if the ratio is used correctly, you can actually increase the amount of behavior that occurs as a result of moving from a continuous to an intermittent reinforcement schedule.

Let's presume we are standing in front of an elevator waiting to go up. The elevator arrives and we walk in. In the afternoon, we walk out of the office and over to the elevator again and push the button. The elevator doesn't come right away so we push the button three times in quick succession. After the third push the elevator does open. Next time in front of the elevator, we push the button, the doors don't open right away so we quickly push the button three more times. The doors still don't open immediately; so you push the button with some degree of irritation about seven or eight times. The elevator door opens. You have learned that if the elevator doesn't come right away, all you have to do is press the button rapidly several more times and usually it comes, although that may not always work. Sometimes you have to push it seven or eight times. Here are the principles at work in this situation:

1. If a previously reinforced behavior is not reinforced, there is a temporary increase in the amount of the behavior.

2. If reinforcement occurs while the rate of response is high (the elevator coming while you were pushing the button many times), future responses will be at the high rate and the high rate will persist for longer periods.

3. If the schedule of reinforcement is progressively stretched out and the intervals made longer, not only very high levels of performance but also very high levels of persistence will be developed.

An interesting experiment in scheduling reinforcement was performed by Edward Pedalino, president of Pedalino and Associates of Ann Arbor, Michigan. The problem tackled was absenteeism in a midwestern manufacturing plant. Called in to help reduce absenteeism, Pedalino found that the union contract actually encouraged absenteeism because of the sick-pay policy of the company. However, there was nothing that could be done about the union contract; it was set in cement. What was needed was more positive consequences for coming to work. A creative individual, Pedalino decided to use a poker game incentive system because of the very visible employee interest in lotteries and raffles. Because of his track record in previous work, management agreed to the plan.

Each day an employee came to work on time, he or she was allowed to choose a card from a deck presented by his or her foreman. At the end of a five-day week, every employee who had come to work on time each day had five cards, or a normal poker hand. The highest hand won $20. There were eight winners, approximately one for each department. Charts were posted on a day-to-day performance basis so that each employee could see how he or she and other employees were doing. The last card in the payoff was given on Sunday, traditionally the day of highest absenteeism in this company.

The program was set up to run in two phases. Phase I was for six weeks, during which time there was a significant decrease in absenteeism.

However, it is one thing to introduce a program that reduces absenteeism, but it is quite another to maintain reduced absenteeism over a period of time. So a second phase, Phase II, was instituted. In contrast to Phase I, it operated only every other week for a period of ten weeks. Nevertheless, absenteeism was considerably lower than what it had been before the program was instituted, although it was slightly higher during the initial phase.

Over a four-month period, 215 unionized employees showed an 18.3 percent reduction in the rate of absenteeism. Over the same period, control groups not participating in the "poker program" actually increased their absenteeism by 13.8 percent.

Moreover, an additional benefit was noted. Since employees not only had to be present but also had to be on time before they could choose their card, a decrease in tardiness also occurred. Also, in terms of reinforcement schedules, it is possible to stretch out schedules of reinforcement and maintain a behavior over extended periods of time. However, a word of warning is in order. Reinforcement schedules cannot be stretched out exceedingly long, particularly

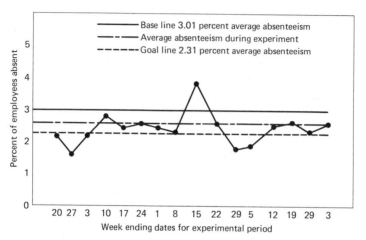

FIGURE 9.1 Effect of poker playing on absenteeism

at the beginning of the stretching process. In the case histories studied above, during the week of October 15 there was an increase in absenteeism from 2.3 to 3.9 percent (see Figure 9.1). Because of circumstances beyond the control of the people conducting the poker program, it was not put into operation during the weeks of October 1, 8, and 15, three weeks in a row. The interval for reinforcement had exceeded the point that could maintain good attendance. When the poker program was reinstituted, absenteeism immediately dropped to 2.4 percent and stayed at about that level for the next six weeks, with the poker program being in operation only every other week.

10

How to Stop Behavior: Punishment and Extinction

In Chapter 9 we examined reinforcement techniques—ways of obtaining the behavior we want on the job. Sometimes these techniques are not enough. Sometimes we want to eliminate a behavior. Here we will examine three methods for getting rid of unwanted behavior.

PUNISHMENT

"Punishment" is a term denoting a precise procedure based upon empirical evidence. It is not torture or physical abuse applied in a random fashion with little concern for behavior patterns or specific behavioral responses. Rather, punishment is an act that follows a specific behavior with another act or event that is presumed to be

143

punishing. If the initial behavior occurs less frequently after this punishment, then the follow-up event or act was a punisher. If, however, the initial event or behavior is followed with a presumed punisher and the initial behavior does not change, the follow-up act is not a punisher.

In order to define something as a punisher, the follow-up event must be related to the initial behavior and must also result in a decrease in that behavior. If the behavior does not decrease, then there has been no punishment.

This example will help illustrate the point. I was walking through a warehouse operation of a firm with which I do some work. One of the fork lift drivers (usually called "jeepers") came by driving a fork-lift truck improperly. As a result of improperly driving, the forks of the truck swung wide around a corner and knocked over a stack of boxes with jars of honey in them. Needless to say, some of the cases fell and opened, and in the fall a number of jars of honey were broken; a sticky mass then began to ooze across the floor. The general foreman immediately rushed over to the scene of the accident and in no uncertain terms chewed out the individual driving the truck. The jeeper nodded contritely and looked ashamed. However, from where I was standing, I could see a number of his colleagues on the other side of the aisle behind the general foreman. They were clasping their hands over their heads, giving the thumbs-up sign, and bent over double with silent laughter. As I walked over to join the general foreman to continue our walk through the warehouse, I glanced back and noticed that the jeeper's friends had crossed the aisle. I could see a lot of hand shaking, back slapping, and laughing. As we walked along the general foreman made several remarks that indicated he felt he had punished the driver. On the other hand, based upon my observations, I felt there had been no punishment.

A couple of weeks later, I was walking through the plant with the same foreman and the same jeeper came zipping by us driving recklessly. "That guy must be just too dumb to remember," said the general foreman. "I must have chewed him out four or five times for driving that way and it doesn't seem to have any effect. I am going to have to give him a verbal warning and see if that will change his driving habits."

My guess is that the driving habits won't change. What this general foreman saw as punishment was not perceived as such by the driver. Remember the definition: punishment occurs only if the follow-up event is related to specific initial behavior and there is a decrease in that behavior as a result of the event. In this case, there was no decrease in the undesired driving behavior of the jeeper.

As you may have guessed, while its use appears simple the use of punishment is considerably more complex than appears on the surface. Yet it is often used. Robert Kreitner of Arizona State University states that punishment is frequently used for three reasons:

1. Punishment works, at least in the short run.
2. Punishment is conveniently used in management by exception.
3. The long-run, undesirable side effects of punishment are generally not known.

If a supervisor yells at employees who are loafing on the job, the employees will quickly get back to work (although they may remain at work only until their supervisor leaves the job area). From this, the supervisor learns that if he or she yells at employees, they will go back to work. The supervisor is "reinforced" for yelling at employees. In the short run, punishment appears to work well. In the long run, this punishment doesn't work.

Management by exception is a technique that is often used with the techniques described in Chapter 5. Under management by exception, the manager establishes the standards of performance, then keeps a watchful eye out for substandard performance. On the surface, this would appear to be an efficient technique for keeping things under control. However, its primary deficiency is that managers become preoccupied with identifying and then punishing performance that is below standard. Experience tells us that the supervisor then tends to overlook or ignore performance that is either good or moving in the right direction and chooses instead to notice only mistakes, which creates a negative job climate.

However, management by exception can be used to develop a positive job climate if the supervisor will look for not one but two types of exceptions. The first type of exception is that when performance goes below standard, rather than punishing the performance the supervisor takes a management posture like the following: "Henry, I see we are below standard. You know that is of concern to me. What can we do to get it back up to where it was?"

The second type of exception is when the employee's performance level changes for the better. If an employee has been averaging 10 units an hour and suddenly moves to an average of 11 units an hour, that's an exception. The exception is to the average of 10; if the manager notes that increase and reinforces the improvement from 10 to 11, then management by exception does not develop the negative climate that generally occurs when only substandard performance is tracked.

Punishment can lead to a number of other long-term problems. People get so they can tolerate punishment up to a point, much like taking medication. When an individual first starts taking medication, its effect is much greater than after taking the medication for five months. Just as a person gets used to a particular drug, an individual can get used to punishment. By analogy, individuals who are consistently poor performers and therefore punished frequently become immune to punishment. Punishment ceases to affect their behavior. Second, the effects of punishment are only temporary unless they are felt continually. Think back to the last time you received a ticket for speeding. You probably drove more slowly for a short time afterward, but gradually your speed level probably increased again. The employee who is continually punished by her supervisor for setting her machine at the wrong rate will always be sure to set the machine at the correct rate when she thinks that the supervisor is in her work area. However, when the supervisor is out of her work area, the behavior of setting the machine at the wrong rate will return. This leads the supervisor into a hectic game of cat and mouse, designed to keep the employee performing at least at a minimum level.

Another problem with punishment is that it tends to eliminate not just the behavior that is being punished but other related behavior as well. If, for example, young employees are criticized for the "dumb suggestions" they submit, they will tend to quit submitting any suggestions or may generalize the punishment even further and stop communicating with their supervisor altogether, even if they are having difficulty running their machines. Sales trainees who are criticized severely and punished for their efforts at overcoming customer objections during a cold sales call will quickly learn that it doesn't pay to make such calls because one is always punished whenever one does.

Punishment also tends to generate excuses. No one likes to be punished or told he or she is doing a poor job. We all try to blame other causes than ourselves for poor performance. Punishment tends to focus on past actions and forces employees to make excuses for past failures rather than concentrate on corrections of the problem in the future.

Disintegration of employee relationships is another often overlooked but undesirable side effect of punishment. The person being punished often gets very angry and comes to dislike the supervisor. This dislike or resentment may not come out in the open, but it is there and hampers the building of effective relationships and communications. Moreover, it often disrupts teamwork and leads team members to dislike not only the supervisor but each other.

Punishment leads to escape and avoidance behavior. Escape behavior occurs when an individual really escapes either the physiological or psychological punishing situation found on a job. The employee whose sales were down last month and who did not show up at the Monday morning meeting is often displaying escape behavior.

Avoidance behavior is much like escape behavior but with one slight difference. As a result of having been punished in the past, people learn to associate certain antecedents with punishment. These antecedents serve as cues for future punishment. For example, avoidance behavior is found in employees who work very hard the week before the monthly meeting because they know that if they don't, they will be punished during that meeting.

Finally, although punishment can stop an undesired behavior from occurring, it does not ensure that the correct behavior will occur. If I punish someone for snapping at a customer, I have not ensured that the sales clerk will do the right thing (smile at a customer, use the customer's name, thank the customer for shopping at our store, etc.). I may have brought about reduced contact by the sales clerk with customers for fear of punishment associated with that event.

WHEN TO USE PUNISHMENT

We don't say that punishment should never be used. On the contrary, it is an essential ingredient in managing human behavior, particularly when we are trying to manage the behavior of a group of individuals in a collective fashion as in a business organization. However, rules and guidelines exist that tell us when to use punishment:

1. Punishment must be used very carefully. Removal of the punishment must be made contingent upon obtaining the desired behavior. That is, the punishment will stop only when the desired behavior occurs on the job.
2. When punishment is used, an alternative, desirable behavior should be available. The only way to avoid punishment must be to perform that desired behavior.
3. Punishment should be consistent and follow every instance of the behavior. It cannot be used in a haphazard or random fashion.

4. Punishment must be used immediately; otherwise the employee may not be sure why the punishment is given.

5. Minimize any attention that goes with the punishment. The attention may inadvertently reinforce the very behavior we are trying to eliminate.

6. Identify in specific terms the behavior being punished. It is not enough to say a person is being punished because he or she has not been persistent. Specify the exact job behaviors that are being punished—where persistence was lacking and the like.

7. When using punishment, talk about job behaviors and not about people. Do not say, "Helen, I am going to punish you because you are lazy and haven't produced enough this last week." Instead say, "Helen, because your job performance has not been up to standard, the system requires me to give you a verbal warning." It is then the system that is punishing Helen, not you. This helps maintain a good personal relationship with the employee and at the same time allows you to punish undesirable behavior.

EXTINCTION

Extinction is an infrequently used and frequently misunderstood way of eliminating undesired employee behavior. Yet it is deceptively simple and effective. Extinction is simply withholding or withdrawing reinforcement that was previously part of a job situation. Let's go back to an earlier example and carry it a little further to show how extinction works.

Recall the example of the jeeper driving down through the warehouse knocking over the case of honey and being reprimanded by the general foreman. Although the general foreman thought he was punishing the jeeper, he was in fact reinforcing his bad driving practices. This happened simply because every time the jeeper drove incorrectly, he received attention for his recklessness. Whatever form the attention took from the general foreman, the jeeper was reinforced not by the foreman but by his colleagues, who clapped, cheered, made the thumbs-up sign, raised hands over their heads, and gave the "v" for victory sign as every case of honey fell to the floor.

In this incident, the use of extinction to change the jeeper's driving behavior would require the general foreman to conduct himself in such a way that the jeeper receives no reinforcement for bad driving practices. This would involve either of two options: (1) ignoring the bad driving practices completely or (2) discussing the driving practices in a manner such that reinforcement from fellow employees would not be forthcoming. This might involve saying to the jeeper, "Tom, I see that the cases are knocked over. As you know, that's of concern to me. What can be done to reduce the number of times this happens?" (This is an example of "supportive confrontation of nonperformance.") Thus, the general foreman has confronted the performance problem but has not done so in a manner that is particularly punishing or reinforcing.

In the clinical setting, it is often possible to ignore behavior completely, especially under closely controlled conditions. However, in the job setting, it is not possible to ignore behavior completely (the true meaning of "extinction"), and we do have to confront nonperformance. Thus, many times in an organization the closest we can come to extinguishing the behavior is to confront that poor performance supportively.

Extinction as the word applies to the job can be seen in the case of Louie, the office comedian. He is always telling jokes, clowning around, and pulling tricks. He is a likeable sort of fellow with a keen sense of humor, a repertoire of good jokes, and the ability to keep everyone in stitches. Unfortunately, he is so busy keeping everyone in stitches that he doesn't have time to do his work. What's worse, the other workers are so busy being in stitches that they don't have time to do their work either. It's not difficult to see why this behavior is occurring. Everyone is laughing and telling Louie, "That's a real screamer," slapping their knees, showering him with reinforcement for his antics. A difficult problem is getting Louie to stop this behavior. Some light-heartedness and joviality around an office is good; it helps keep tension down and break up the work routine. If the supervisor moves in too hard on Louie and tells him to stop telling jokes, he may generate a great deal of antagonism on Louie's part, who will then grumble that the supervisor has no sense of humor and was never any good anyway. Louie will then continue telling jokes but not when the supervisor is around. A more effective technique to induce Louie to stop telling so many jokes in the office is simply not to laugh at the jokes. Do nothing, not even smile. That will change the joke-telling behavior better and more quickly than verbal punishment. Moreover, the other employees will realize that perpetual joke telling is not appropriate and will stop laughing at Louie.

Another clear-cut example of extinction can be seen in the child who throws tantrums in the drugstore to get an ice cream cone. Typically, this child is already on an intermittent reinforcement schedule. She doesn't get an ice cream cone every time she cries, just once out of every four or five times. If you recall the chapter on schedules of reinforcement, you may remember that an intermittent reinforcement schedule is the one that produces the highest level of behavior we are trying to reinforce. Punishing this child does no good. All she will do is scream more and go back to yelling for an ice cream cone. In part, the punishment is another form of attention for her, so she is getting reinforcement whether or not she gets the ice cream. If she does get it, she is reinforced for throwing a tantrum; and if her mother scolds and spanks her, that won't do; she is getting attention, which no doubt reinforces this behavior. The easiest way to cure the child of throwing tantrums is to ignore them. This is easier said than done, but it is nevertheless the only sure way of doing it. Moreover, it is the quickest. Here is what the parent should do. As soon as the child starts throwing the tantrum, ignore her altogether.

Then watch out. First the behavior increases, the frequency, duration, and intensity of the tantrums increases. In the case of our office clown, the story telling, antics, and practical joking increase. Why? For the same reason that when we stood in front of the elevator, pushed the button, and it didn't come, we pushed the button several more times in quick succession. In all three examples, the same principle is at work. When a previously reinforced behavior is no longer reinforced (extinction), the amount of that behavior temporarily goes up. For this reason, it is critical that the extinction, or ignoring of behavior, remains firm. If the parent reinforces the child who is throwing the tantrum, if we reinforce Louie for telling a joke, or if the elevator comes when we push the button three times in quick succession, that new and higher level of behavior, more frequent behavior, will continue. It is thus imperative that extinction continue, for if the individual is reinforced for joke telling, crying, or pushing the button, he or she is on an intermittent reinforcement schedule, and that one bit of reinforcement is enough to keep that behavior going. However, if the behavior is simply ignored and no reinforcement is forthcoming, the behavior very quickly extinguishes itself. It does not, for example, take long for the candy machine to extinguish the behavior of inserting the dime. It happened in two days. If, on the other hand, the machine gave the candy bar after the second time, nothing after the next time, two candy bars after the next time, nothing for the next two times, then one candy bar, then two candy bars, then nothing for three more times in succession, then two candy bars, and so on, soon all the employees in the company would cluster around the machine trying to hit the jackpot. They would be on an intermittent reinforcement schedule and their behavior would be very similar to that of people who play slot machines. This is why it is important not to reinforce the behavior at all. This prescription is an extremely difficult behavior on the part of the supervisor. If a supervisor gives any sign at all (smile, frown, shaking the head, walking away in disgust, hitting his forehead with his hand), it is very often enough to reinforce that behavior. Unintentionally, the supervisor has put that employee on an intermittent reinforcement schedule. It is then necessary only to shake his head every six or seven times to maintain that same undesired behavior.

REINFORCING INCOMPATIBLE BEHAVIORS

A final technique for getting rid of undesired behavior is to reinforce the behavior that is incompatible with the behavior we don't want. If, for example, an employee is coming to work late and we want her or him to come to work on time, we can reinforce coming to work on time. This leads to a decrease in the number of times the employee comes to work late. Here is another example of reinforcing incompatible behavior. If Louie, the office clown, spends most of his time telling jokes and his antics are disturbing the office routine, we can reinforce behaviors that are incompatible with the joke telling. If the supervisor walks by Louie's desk and finds him busy at work, the supervisor can reinforce that behavior by saying, "Say, Louie, I see you are working on the Jones file. That's really great because I know we have to have it completed by closing time this afternoon. I really appreciate the extra effort you are putting into it." In doing this, the supervisor has reinforced the behavior—Louis's working hard at his desk—that is incompatible with the undesired behavior of clowning around. As a result of the reinforcement, the amount of clowning around will diminish and the amount of time spent at the desk working hard will increase. Thus, for every undesired behavior we want to eliminate, there is usually, if not always, a desired behavior we want to increase. If we are able to reinforce the behavior that is incompatible with the undesired behavior, we can increase the amount of desirable behavior and thereby decrease the amount incompatible behavior.

11

Key Ingredients in Developing Behavior - Change Programs

Making techniques such as those described in this book work in practice is quite different from reading about them in a book. In working with organizations in a variety of areas, including manufacturing, sales, warehousing, quality control, health care, marketing, distribution, and the like, I have observed some important factors that strongly affect behavior-change projects that use the techniques described in this book.

"Skill training" is one of these factors. For individuals who will be involved in changing employee behavior, skill-building workshops are imperative in the techniques of analyzing human performance problems, designing effective feedback systems, using positive reinforcement, selecting appropriate reinforcers, as well as overview of these concepts. The key ingredient is the word "skill." This book develops the concepts and shows you what the techniques are, but your reading the book is not a workshop session. Because you have read this book, we can be pretty sure you will know what the skills and techniques are. However, we can not be sure you can implement those skills or that you will feel comfortable coaching other members of their staff in applying them. Most people readily accept the concepts developed in this book; by the same token, most people also find that they need further skill development to be able effectively to apply and refine the system described here.

In an ideal skill-building workshop, the people who intend to apply the techniques should go back to their job situations with a specific behavior-change project they have outlined during the course of the workshop. Establishing take-home projects for participants during the workshop increases both the probability that one will actually put the system to work as well as the likelihood of success on the project. When a workshop participant goes home with an action plan in hand, he or she advances beyond the head-nodding stage of "Boy, that was great." "Yeah, it really was interesting." "Those techniques sure seem to work; well, what should we do now?" "I don't know. Let's go back to the things we were doing before." Our experience has been a 60 to 70 percent success rate with projects worked out and taken home from workshops. This success rate increases the long-term usage of the technology since people become accustomed to using it.

SELECTION OF APPROPRIATE PROJECTS

People exposed to the techniques described in this book often suffer initially from something that one organizational consultant calls the "little boy with the hammer" syndrome: give a small boy a hammer and he thinks everything is for hammering—wooden blocks, carpeting, radiators, walls, windows, pots and pans, daddy's toe, mommy's hand, and big sister's tennis racket. In this situation, give a supervisor a tool or technology that he or she knows will work, sees work, understands how it works, and it's like turning the small boy loose with the hammer. He thinks everything is for applying behavioral analysis. While many (I would even venture to say most) human performance situations can be improved with the use of the techniques described in this book, the overenthusiasm that accompanies the little boy with the hammer syndrome tends to lead people to select projects that are too big or complex for their first project. In the workshop, when people begin to select projects, they invariably try to tackle something that is considerably larger in scope than they are ready to handle. They want to solve all production control problems, all marketing problems, all distribution problems, all manufacturing problems, all quality control problems. They want to have a dramatic effect on the bottom line performance of the organization within a three-month period.

We recommend against this. Behavioral analysis in its most systematic application is a new technology for most managers and supervisors. To fully refine and develop their skills in this area, these people need time to practice and apply them in a variety of situations. Success in and of itself serves as a reinforcer, and that reinforcement comes sooner with a shorter-term project. Once a manager has accomplished two or three successful and relatively small projects, with goals accomplished in a relatively short time (one to three months) he or she is more apt to have the patience to wait out the results on a 6-to-12-month project. If an individual goes back and tackles a project that will be six, eight, or more months in showing results, there is a higher probability of losing interest in the techniques simply because the results have not come quickly enough.

Understandably, most long-term projects are more difficult and complex than shorter-term projects. It is better for employees to "cut their teeth" on these shorter-term projects in order to gain experience with the use of the technology. Rather than trying to solve all the quality control problems in the next two months, we suggest narrowing the project to, for instance, rework or rejects or customer returned material. Tackling one of these is a good way to begin applying some of the techniques described. Once rework in a particular department is controlled and at a completely satisfactory level, we can then turn attention to rework in another department and then successively to other departments. Once rework is under control in all departments, the employee can then turn attention to scrap, and when scrap is under control in all departments, then quality control is under control. It might take ten or perhaps even 12 months to achieve results in the entire quality control area, but the probability of that is much greater if the areas selected for improvement are picked off one at a time. Don't try to tackle the whole world at once.

AVOIDING THE FAD EFFECT

In recent years, we have witnessed the entire range of business cure-alls from the managerial grid, sensitivity training, job enrichment, transactional analysis, hula hoops, and skateboards. In the next few years, the use of behavioral technology, and particularly positive reinforcement, could become regarded as a fad. The difference is that even if used as a fad, behavioral technology works, but only as long as it continues to be utilized. For those organizations where the techniques described in this book are regarded as a fad, the techniques will work only for a short period of time, and then the organization will try something else, perhaps "transactional analysis," "job enrichment," or "MBO goes to the seashore." If the techniques become a short term fad, they will not prove a particularly long-term benefit to the organization.

The techniques described in this book are useful not only in changing employee behavior, but in ensuring that behavior is maintained over an extended period of time. The use of these techniques cannot become merely an addition to the manager's job; they must be part of the way that manager manages. Only in that way will they benefit the organization over the long term. The job of manager is to manage the performance of the organization under his or her area of responsibility. The techniques give the manager the tools for doing just that. In short, the job of the manager is overseeing the total performance system for which he or she is held accountable.

WILLINGNESS TO TOLERATE SETBACKS

The use of behavioral technology in business and industry works and works well. It pays off on the bottom line and is an extremely powerful technology that can be used for changing employee behavior. Dramatic and lasting changes in absenteeism, cost control, safety, tardiness, customer relations, quality, production, productivity, error rate, and other performance areas have been obtained in such diverse organizations as manufacturing, warehousing, sales, retailing, health care, wholesaling-distribution, and restaurant operations. However, the techniques do not always work; they are not infallible, and sometimes short-term or even long-term setbacks may occur. For example, reinforcers in a system are sometimes impossible to change that more than offset anything an individual or group can do to overcome them. Sometimes inappropriate reinforcers are selected (a key ingredient of a workshop is helping participants to select the appropriate reinforcer), and the wrong behavior on the part of employees is elicited for a short time.

Although behavioral technology is a good, it is not foolproof. We who apply this technique have on occasion experienced both small and once in a while large setbacks. It is true of human beings that we sometimes make errors in predicting the exact effects of changes. This in turn affects the system of behavior technology we're discussing. The fault lies, of course, not with the system or the use of the technology, but rather with the application of the technology by an individual manager or consultant. The firm that seeks to apply the techniques described in this book should expect good results. The results should be demonstrable and directly related to training sessions and to implementation of the techniques, but the firm must also be willing to tolerate some short-term setbacks in any series of performance improvement projects.

COMMITMENT FROM THE TOP OF THE APPROPRIATE ORGANIZATIONAL UNIT

To make the techniques we've described work well, it is important to have commitments from the top of the appropriate organizational unit. This does not mean that there has to be commitment to the techniques from the chairman of the board or the president of the firm. It does mean, however, that if we are going to use the techniques and apply them in the area of manufacturing, there has to be commitment from the vice president of operations and the vice president of manufacturing or the director of manufacturing—whatever that title happens to be. It is, of course, helpful if there is commitment and involvement across the board from all areas of the company. But company-wide commitment is not essential. In fact, in some firms with which I have worked either on project implementation or training sessions, we have worked with only one area, say, warehousing and distribution or manufacturing. The results in those areas where we worked had a clearly demonstrable payoff on the bottom line. There was no initial support from other areas of the firm for use of the techniques, so that initially the manufacturing area, for example, was pretty much on its own. As results from implemented projects became known throughout the company, however, other areas of the firm became interested and then involved in the use of the technology. In many instances, we have moved into other areas of the firm once the results started to be known from the initial project. However, we make such moves only where we have the active support and involvement of the head of that particular area.

It is not enough for a manager to say, "This sounds like good stuff. It's something that the people who work for me should practice more of." That manager must use the techniques described in this book with the members of his or her staff. It is foolish to expect lower levels of management to practice reinforcement techniques if those same individuals are not themselves reinforced. This tends to lead to fairly short-term application of the reinforcement techniques. The refrain of lower-level managers soon becomes, "They want me to reinforce the machine operators, but nobody ever reinforces me." That statement clearly indicates that the application of the technology will not be for very long. Thus, it is important for top management to communicate clearly their intent to follow through on individual systems and projects. This intent to follow through must come not only in the form of verbal intent—"We think these are good techniques and intend to use them"—but must also be clearly communicated through management practices. It must be "do as I do." It cannot be the old "do as I say and not as I do" syndrome.

DEVELOPMENT BY LINE MANAGEMENT

The techniques described in this book must be practiced by line management. They cannot be just a personnel program. If behavior-change projects are approved by, started by, channeled through, or monitored by employee relations, training, or some other similar staff function, the techniques will become labeled "another one of those things those crazys in personnel or training dreamed up." They will not be labeled "a management technique that we here in line management use because it helps us get better bottom-line performance." This is not to suggest that the employee relations staff should not be involved in the application of these techniques. They should be involved, and the maximum benefit is derived when they are involved. Staff employees can participate effectively, for instance, in conducting the skill training sessions and serving in this capacity either to conduct the sessions themselves or to coinstruct with the use of an outside resource person. Moreover, personnel, employee relations, and training people are usually well versed in many of the techniques described in this book and can serve as "internal change agents" by providing the follow-up counseling to employees who are applying the techniques described.

Another important involvement of line managers in applying these techniques is as trainers or instructors in workshop sessions. In one firm, for example, where we have worked on attendance control and employee productivity, one of the line managers served as a trainer during some of the workshops for lower levels of management. This individual had been through a previous workshop and had applied some of the techniques in his area of operation. As we moved to other areas of the firm in the application of techniques, he served as an instructor in the workshop, thus adding even more credibility to the techniques by describing how he used them and the results he had obtained. He was in effect our Wheaties commercial, saying, "I eat behavioral technology for breakfast and it helps my department grow strong."

PATIENCE IN OBTAINING RESULTS

Results derived from these techniques usually begin to make themselves known at least partially within four to six weeks after the techniques are applied. Many times, however, real results are two to four months in coming. In one firm, for example, we began the analytical phase of a project in November and continued it through January. The training was conducted in December, and although some results began to show in January, the real effect became apparent in May and June as accumulative results of the efforts over the preceding months began to work together. As mentioned earlier, not all implementation on the projects works out exactly as planned. There is often a need for modification and corrective action on problem projects. Problems become apparent at this point as there is often some dropoff in initial enthusiasm. Supervisors become aware that these techniques, while they are effective management tools and can be used too dramatically to improve employee performance, are not a panacea and do not provide cook book recipes for short cuts to success.

RELATIONSHIPS TO STANDARDS OF PERFORMANCE AND BREAKTHROUGH OBJECTIVES

Organizations that already have a goal-setting program will find that the techniques of behavior change described in this book serve as an active support to that goal-setting system. Many organizations have in fact worked these behavior-change techniques into existing management by objectives systems. If you do not have some type of goal-setting system, it is important to agree on the basic status performance for each job within the organization. Managers must communicate those areas in which they have strong feelings about basic standards. In areas where performance falls below standard, it is imperative to set objectives to get performance back up to standard. In job areas where performance is already at standard or exceeding it, it is still advisable to establish some breakthrough objectives to see whether employees can raise performance above its present level.

The key to remember is that the use of positive reinforcement and positive feedback should not prevent a manager from confronting nonperformance. In fact, the techniques of this book demand that managers confront nonperformance. The main difference between these techniques and traditional management techniques is that the former confront nonperformance supportively rather than berating employees for poor performance. The manager using the techniques of this book confronts the area of nonperformance, thanks employees for keeping accurate records about job performance, asks employees what can be done to improve performance, and finally, provides reinforcement for continued improvement in performance. Thus, the manager is not prevented from rediscussing standards that were initially agreed upon as the minimum acceptable level for a job when performance falls below that level. The key difference is that in our system, the manager now has a technique for bringing performance not only up to the minimum standard but carrying it beyond that standard.

SUBORDINATE INVOLVEMENT IN PROJECTS

If you apply the techniques in this book, it is helpful to involve your subordinates as much as possible in the development of performance improvement projects for a number of reasons. First, your subordinates are often closest to the situation and can provide very relevant information for the performance problem at hand. They are the ones often on the firing line and can make or break a performance improvement project. This doesn't mean you should not contribute information you possess that you feel is applicable to the situation; from where you stand, you have a somewhat different perspective and should be able to contribute significant information that will be useful and, by all means, applicable in the development of performance improvement projects.

The techniques of behavior change are not mysterious tools that you can not share with your subordinates. They are practical tools your subordinates should use in helping the people who report to them improve performance.

DATA COLLECTION

As you begin to use some of these techniques, you will no doubt recognize the need for revision in your information systems. It is helpful to build in automatic feedback directly for those who need the information to make decisions and take corrective action. One of the easiest ways to do this, of course, is to examine the data of those whose behavior is being measured. Although it might also be necessary to have an outside control to make sure that that data collection is accurate, it helps (for reasons described in Chapter 10) to have those individuals measure their own behavior. A word of caution: do not build too much feedback into the system. A convenient number of measures for an employee to keep track of is usually no more than six or seven. If much more feedback than this amount is built into the system, it typically ends up being more than a subordinate can handle. What happens is that instead of focusing improvement efforts in those six or seven areas, the employee tries to shotgun efforts and ends up doing nothing very well.

THE HAWTHONE EFFECT

The Hawthone Effect is part of the folklore of behavior science and management practices. It is based upon studies done at a Western Electric Company plant that manufactured equipment for the Bell Telephone System. The folklore surrounding the Hawthone plant suggests that the studies initially tried to determine how changes in illumination would effect the production rate of female employees who inspected parts, assembled relays, or wound coils. In most instances, the employees were reported to have worked faster regardless of changes in illumination. It has become common practice to refer to this effect as the "Hawthone Effect." It has also been used to suggest that no matter what change you make in a given management situation, the Hawthone Effect takes place and changes will occur. However, H. M. Parsons,[1] of the Institute for Behavioral Research, has pointed out not only that are there several holes in assumptions currently held about the Hawthone Effect, but also that it is possible to explain what happened by using the principles of behavioral technology.

Investigation into the original research suggests several things. First, the generally held assumptions about the Hawthone experiments are not accurate. Although most writers who mention the Hawthone Effect describe it as a single study, in fact seven such studies took place between 1924 and 1932. During those seven studies and in contrast to what is popularly reported, other factors besides illumination were changed. Many of these changes can be explained in terms of behavioral technology. Most of the increases in employee productivity can be accounted for by examining the changes and how they relate to behavioral technology. One of the primary changes, for instance, was in the pay structure. Previously the workers, all female employees, had been paid on a complicated piecework system that tied individual performance into departmental performance. Each employee received a guaranteed hourly wage and then a sum based upon the amount by which total departmental production exceeded certain standards. Under the conditions of the experiment, the entire department group of 100 was reduced to a group of five. Then each employee's earnings were based upon the amount by which the productivity of the five employees exceeded their collective hourly wages. Because of the reduction in unit size from 100 to 5, the payment was more directly proportional to individual efforts.

Moreover, to collect data on production rate in the test room, a special method was developed. Each completed relay was dropped down a chute next to the operator. When a flap was opened by a relay, that was recorded. A separate counter was maintained for each operator who accumulated the total number of completed relays. The counters were visible to any operator at any time she wished to look at them. Readings were taken from the counters every half hour. At the end of each day, a report identified the number of relays each worker had completed and the type of relay, the total time for a set of 50, and the time breaks. Another record showed the parts rejected by the operator as well as the number of defective relays assembled, inspected, and returned to the production area. Although it is not known specifically when, how, or how often the operators received information about their performance, it is clear that the information was available to them merely by looking at the counters or the half-hour totals.

More importantly, however, clues about the information use of feedback by the individual operators could be gathered from the original experiment data. For example, late in the afternoon of April 19, 1929, operator 3 said, "I'm about 15 relays behind yesterday." Operator 5 said, "I made 421 yesterday and I am going to do better today." These comments suggest several things. First, there was some type of standard or target that the individual employees had in mind, even if they had not been identified by management. It also suggests that the employees were making use of feedback information. While there is nothing in our investigation that proves that positive reinforcement was used (unintentionally in this situation, since the technique was unknown as a system at that time), it is safe to assume that it was.

In one instance in a hospital, an EKG technician doubled his average hourly output of tracings from 2.5 to 5. The techniques used in this improvement are described in Chapter 8 and 9. Suffice it to say that it consisted of a performance graph combined with reinforcement from supervisory personnel. One of the curious things about the effect of the graph was that staff physicians unaware of the techniques of positive reinforcement commented by making such statements as "from $2\frac{1}{2}$ to $4\frac{1}{2}$ tracings per hour is quite an improvement" without prompting and perhaps without realizing a full impact of their comments upon improvements in the production rate.

In many organizations using graphs, people not even fully aware of the techniques are led to comment favorably on improvements simply because they are looking for something nice to say. They tend not to comment on drops in performance since they don't want to enter into conflict with another department. They are thus combining positive reinforcement with extinction, two of the most powerful techniques we have discussed for changing human behavior. Although I can't prove it from original source data, it is not at all difficult to imagine one of the experimenters or supervisors walking up to operator 4, looking at the counter that records the number of relays produced that was in sight of both the supervisor and the operator, and saying, "Karen, I see your production has gone from 415 a week to an average of 421 a week. That's really great. I'm glad to see that the extra effort you are putting into this experiment is paying off." It is not too difficult to imagine an experimenter or supervisor noticing that Karen's production had dropped one week and then not saying anything but instead rushing away to a conference room to talk with somebody else about what changes were made in illumination that might have affected that change in Karen's job performance. It is not difficult to imagine that the experimenters and supervisors thus unwittingly combined what we now know about feedback systems and how they affect human performance with the application of positive reinforcement and extinction in producing what has come to be known as the Hawthone Effect.

Many organizations that examine the results of behavioral technology or the techniques described in this book and their application to their own situation say the following: these techniques might make sense over the short run, but they are really just an instance of the Hawthone Effect and probably will bring about no lasting change. I might agree that the Hawthone Effect or a change in anything at all may lead to some improvement. However, the Hawthone Effect as popularly described does not lead to documented changes that last over extended periods of time, yet behavioral technology does.

If an individual is willing to describe the Hawthone Effect as an efficient, effective use of feedback systems, as a basis for combining reinforcement with extinction and being sure to move from continuous reinforcement to intermittent reinforcement once a behavior pattern has been developed, then I am willing to agree that the Hawthone Effect does take place. However, under those circumstances, the Hawthone Effect, if one wishes to describe it in terms of behavioral technology, is not a short-term but rather a long-term effect and not at all the one that has become part of the mythology of human relations.

12

Applications

We have described here some of the performance problems that organizations face today and have suggested that the use of a systems model is a useful tool in analyzing and diagnosing human performance problems. We have also suggested that there are five basic reasons why people do not perform as they are supposed to in the organization. Let us briefly review these now in light of the total structure presented in the book.

We examined the use of set standards, goals, and objectives in eliciting desired behavior from employees. Many times employees in organizations do not perform satisfactorily simply because they do not know what is expected of them. As managers, we must define our expectations in terms of job results.

Training is essential. The key question in reference to this is can the employee perform as you desire if his or her job or life depended upon it. If the answer is "Yes, he or she can perform this way but is not," the solution is in another area than training. However, if the person can not perform correctly even if job or life depends upon it, the solution lies in the design of training programs and in the implications of training as a behavior-change agent.

Behavioral consequences are important. We learned how to examine human behavior in much the same way as an old time pharmacist weighs chemicals on a scale. If the scale tips in one direction, we get the behavior we want; if it tips in the other direction, we get undesired job behavior.

We examined the relation of information theory and feedback systems to changing employee behavior. We suggested that feedback that is specific, immediate, and directly related to a target helps employees improve their performance just as yardline markers help a football player measure his progress toward the goal line. Feedback helps employees measure their progress toward goals or objectives.

Reinforcement theory from the area of behavioral psychology is important to apply. We saw how providing reinforcement at the appropriate time not only helps employees to improve job performance, but also gives them added incentives to maintain that higher performance level for extended periods of time. We also saw how moving from a continuous schedule of reinforcement to an intermittant one helps employees maintain desired behavior over an extended period of time.

We examined methods and techniques for obtaining specific behaviors, and we examined punishment and extinction as ways of eliminating undesired behavior. We know that punishment works only under certain conditions. Extinction works better than punishment in eliminating undesired behavior.

Having looked at each of these, a reader might easily conclude that each of these considerations operates separately from the others. In reality, this is not true. They are inextricably intertwined with one another.

Many times people like me are called in as "company doctors" to develop behavior-change programs for a particular firm or department within a firm. When acting in this capacity, we are required by our role to write "behavior-change prescriptions," usually working in concert with the company's trainers, internal-change agents, as well as line managers. We find that the required prescription usually means calling into force several if not all the elements described above (objectives, training, changing consequences, feedback, combining reinforcement with either punishment or extinction). Let's look at some representative case histories to see how these techniques have been applied in different situations and how you might generate ideas for yourself in improving human performance in your organization.

QUALITY CONTROL

Jacobsen Manufacturing Company is a multimillion-dollar company in the commercial and consumer grounds maintenance business. One device the vice president of operations uses in managing manufacturing operations is called a quality performance report. Items included in this report include scrap, rework due to a variety of causes, inspection costs, quality control costs, and salvage labor. In the bottom right corner of the report is an all important number. That number shows quality performance as a percentage of direct labor dollars. Whereas the quality performance report indicated satisfactory performance, it was believed that the company could sharpen its practices even more in this area.

Many areas in quality control can be directly related to human performance problems. Quality control departments and manufacturing engineers can design line operations that help the quality control process of the manufacturing operation. They can build jigs and fixtures that increase the probability of people's producing good parts, and they can monitor operations to ensure that things are as they should be from a technical point of view. However, production managers, quality control managers, and manufacturing engineers are not behavioral psychologists and are sometimes unaware of tools and techniques that can be used to ensure that the organization performs as it should. This is true primarily because the use of behavioral technology in business and industry is a new technique, applied in business and industry only since the 1960s. Thus, the manager who understands the full implication in the applications of behavioral technology in his or her organization is the exception rather than the rule in today's business world. The managers at Jacobsen were such an exception. Good managers skilled in traditional management practices with an effectively and efficiently running organization, they were also competent in understanding the technical aspects of the job. Most importantly through a workshop and follow-up help, they became skillful in the use of behavior technology. The use of the techniques described in this book do not replace effective management practices such as planning, delegating, organizing, and the like. Rather, it gives a manager already applying these techniques a way of implementing them and making them even more efficient.

Moreover, the use of the techniques described herein is not a cure for poor management practices; rather it is a tool for sharpening management practices that are already good.

Because of the scope of the operation at Jacobsen, three primary phases were undertaken:

1. An analytical phase that involved looking at the areas in which improvement would be sought, examining desired performance, and establishing standards and objectives where they were unclear or hazy. This required examining the actual performance of individuals in relation both to desired and required performance and from that determining the performance discrepancy. The causes of the discrepancy between actual and desired performance were then analyzed using the tools described in Chapter 6.

2. A skill-building training session phase was initiated for management supervisory personnel once the causes of the performance deficiency had been analyzed and converted into potential dollar returns (the total potential return in this case was approximately $1 million). A two-day skill-building workshop was conducted for key management personnel and at later dates one-day briefing sessions for supervisory employees were held.

3. An implementation phase was scheduled as soon as the training sessions were completed. Here, solutions to the performance discrepancies were initiated. Working with internal contacts within the company, outside consultants introduced a variety of steps involving the specific solutions to performance problems described in Chapters 5 through 10. Support from everybody in the organization including quality control department personnel, vice president of operations, and first line supervisors was received and found to be not only helpful but, more importantly, it played a critical role in the implementation of the solutions. Wherever possible, employees in the operating departments were directly involved in the change; this was found to pay off not only in bringing the change about, but also in ensuring that implemented solutions were employed over an extended period of time.

Here are some of the key things that were done at Jacobsen. One involved the quality performance report. As a feedback mechanism, it met the needs of upper management in giving them an overall view of what was happening in quality control. However, as an operating document and feedback mechanism, it was seriously deficient. There was no way, for example, for the welding department to determine either what their scrap was as a percentage of direct labor or what their rework was as a percentage of direct labor dollars. So one of the first steps taken was to change the information gathering and feedback system used in this particular situation. Scrap and rework information was fed directly to the cost center responsible for it. Although supervisors in charge of each cost center had a general idea of their performance (i.e., we are doing pretty well, we are doing okay, we are doing pretty poorly), they now had specific information on their scrap and rework performance.

The changes in the feedback system combined with the analytical work done earlier resulted in an interesting phenomenon. Scrap appeared almost to double in the first month of the project. The reason for this was quite simple. The analysis showed that actual scrap was reported approximately twice as scrap. For every piece of scrap reported, another piece of scrap went unreported. This is a common occurrence in many organizations. The cause of reported versus unreported scrap can be explained by behavioral technology. What usually happens when an employee turns in a scrap piece is that he or she is chewed out and punished. The conversation goes something like this: "Mr. Supervisor, I'm afraid I made a bad piece here and I have to turn it in to be scrap." "You idiot, if I've told you once, I've told you a hundred times, we can't produce scrap here. Now get back to your machine and work harder."

The result of this, of course, is that the employee learns that it doesn't pay to report scrap. The only thing that happens when you report scrap is that somebody gets angry. At Jacobsen, however, as a result of the skill-training workshop, supervisors were able to see how *proper* use of reinforcement techniques can be used not only to get people to report scrap accurately but also, and more importantly, to do their part to help get the scrap problem under control. After the skill training, supervisors were more likely to be involved in a situation like this: "Mr. Supervisor, I'm afraid I have to report a scrap." "Mike, I appreciate your reporting the scrap. It's important to us to keep accurate records so that we can know when we have to tackle a problem. However, as you may remember, we discussed this last week and we are concerned about reducing the scrap. What do you think we could do to keep scrap down under one-half of 1 percent of direct labor hours?"

When the employee replied with an appropriate answer, he was again reinforced by the supervisor.

Much of the feedback provided here was not only in the form of numbers on the quality performance report, but also in the form of graphs as described in Chapter 8. If you walk through the various offices and shop areas at Jacobsen now, a representative sample of graphs you might see would include total cost of quality as a percentage of direct labor dollars, total scrap, scrap by department, rework by each department, total rework, and other information that people in operating positions can use to make everyday decisions.

Another representative effect of the behavior-change techniques that came out of Jacobsen are in the area of vendor relations. Most vendors are screamed at when they don't perform and then ignored when they do (their behavior is quickly extinguished). Using the techniques from the workshop and those described in this book, purchasing and manufacturing began to work together more closely to use reinforcement techniques on vendors. Although substandard performance was still noted and dealt with, vendors were also pleasantly surprised (some, I might add, shocked) at receiving a phone call or a note thanking them for improving the quality of their vended parts from an acceptance rate of 98.5 to 99.1 percent. The quality of purchased parts also improved as a result of the applications of some of these techniques. In some firms with which I have worked, including some wholesaler-distributors, not only is the information fed back and improvements noted and reinforced, but the firms maintain graphs for the manufacturer, thus adding one more important element to the feedback system.

Another phase of implementation involving feedback in reinforcement systems involves purchasing and receiving personnel. As part of the implementation steps to improved vendor performance, specific goals were established for the percentage of shipments checked. Each of three vended categories ("a" priority, "b" priority, or "c" priority) and feedback systems were established to allow not only receiving personnel to monitor their own performance (thus providing a basis for reinforcement by supervisory personnel) but also a feedback system from purchasing to receiving to help receiving personnel translate their efforts into dollars for the company. Thus, on a regular basis, receiving room personnel sent off a list of checked shipments to purchasing, which totaled up with a note stating where the shipments were short or long beyond prescribed limits; then purchasing fed back to receiving room personnel data on how much money they had saved the company that week by finding the short shipments. As the productivity of receiving went up in terms of shipments checked, these improvements were reinforced by various management supervisory personnel.

While these are by no means all the steps implemented by this firm, they are representative of some of the different goals established, feedback systems installed, and reinforcement used. Savings have been well worth the efforts that went into the project. On an annualized basis, Jacobsen is realizing savings at approximately $400,000 a year. Although management feels that the efforts will also have a long-term benefit in warranty costs and field service campaigns, these are not expected to show up for several more years. It is not possible to relate directly any changes that far into the future to the efforts that went into this earlier project. Other performance improvements that came about as a result of the changes implemented include fewer line delays due to increased availability of quality parts; better working relationships between departments; more aggressive problem tackling by employees.

SALES IMPROVEMENT

One of the items measured by the operating companies of the Bell System is sales results expressed as total items sold as a percentage of opportunities to sell. In January 1974, one of the companies was not doing well; it ranked sixteenth out of the 20 Bell System companies. However, by January 1975, they were 11 out of 19, and by January 1976, they were 8 out of 19. The reason for this jump in relative ranking since January 1974 is a simple one. In 1974, when many of the other Bell System companies were maintaining a sales average of more than 100 percent, this firm was maintaining a sales average of approximately 80 percent. Determined to improve this percentage, the general commercial supervisor enlisted an outside consultant to help improve sales. Based upon discussions within the company with the outside consultant and careful observation of on-the-job behavior, training emphasizing the material covered in Chapters 5, 8, and 9 (goal setting, feedback, and reinforcement) was conducted for key managers and supervisors. The primary content covered during the skill-building workshops was techniques of goal setting; the proper design and use of feedback systems; and techniques of positive reinforcement.

As a result of the workshops and of the newly acquired skills, several changes were made in management practices that had a dramatic impact on sales. First, there had always been some goal setting, but the new goal setting was not only very specific but the goal-setting cycle was shortened. Previously, goals had been established in a somewhat haphazard fashion for a period of six months to a year.

Goal setting (depending upon the level in the organization) was shortened considerably. The top of the organization still had quarterly and annual goals; however, as goal setting made its way down the organization chart, the cycle was shortened considerably. At the first line of supervision, goal setting became a monthly event. For the service representative (the person who actually made contact with the customer and made the sale), the goal-setting cycle ranged from one day to one month. For most of the service representatives, the time covered by the goal was somewhere between one week and one month. However, for problem employees, new employees, or any individual whose performance was only marginal, the goal-setting cycle was shortened to one day. Thus, an employee experiencing sales difficulty was set a target for each day.

Combined with the shortened goal-setting cycles were shortened feedback cycles. Feedback had previously been on a monthly basis, when computer printouts were made available. For someone working in sales, getting needed daily feedback on a monthly feedback basis is of little or no value. Although the monthly computer printouts were continued, most offices shortened the feedback cycle to daily or weekly basis—depending upon the performance level of the individual employee. Employees who were performing well received weekly feedback. What they received was not a long, complicated, appraisal interview but simply information on how they were doing. Again, for marginal employees, the feedback cycle was shortened to one day and in a few cases to even an effort-by-effort basis.

The importance of the shortened feedback cycle is critical for it shortens the success interval for an individual employee. Take, for example, the case of a salesperson whose sales efforts were at a level of 60 percent. To increase sales performance to 100 percent would seem virtually impossible. However, by shortening both the goal-setting and feedback cycles, the somewhat larger task was broken down into a series of smaller steps that brought them closer and closer to the 100 percent level, thus giving an opportunity for some success on a regular basis even if there wasn't success every time. A service representative at 60 percent, for example, might establish the goal of 65 percent for tomorrow. When he reached 65 percent, his goal would be increased to 67 percent. From 67 percent, it goes to 70 percent, and before long, performance is at 100 percent or higher.

The third change was increased use of positive reinforcement. In particular, heavy use was made of shaping. Employees already performing well (100 percent sales or better) were reinforced on an intermittent basis or maintained that level with somewhat more frequent but still intermittent reinforcement. The results of these efforts are not surprising. The top performers improved. Because they were already performing at a high level, their performance increase was not as dramatic (i.e., doubling or tripling) as was that of some of the lower performance personnel. Nevertheless the increase was substantial. In many cases, service representatives performing at the 110 to 120 percent level were able to increase their performance to closer to 140 or 160 percent.

The most dramatic improvements came, however, with individuals whose performance was below 100 percent. If their performance level was substantially below 100 percent (i.e., around 50 or 60 percent), improvements were not only substantial but in most instances dramatic. Heavy use of positive reinforcement was made with these individuals. Here is how.

Let's suppose someone was performing at 60 percent and that at a goal-setting session with his supervisor, a target of 65 percent was established for the next day. Several things could happen in relation to that target:

1. It could be surpassed, going to 67, 68, or 69 percent or even higher.
2. The target could be hit exactly—65 percent.
3. The employee could increase performance tomorrow somewhere between the present level and the target (somewhere between 60 and 65 percent).
4. Performance could remain at 60 percent.
5. Performance tomorrow could be worse than today (less than 60 percent).

No matter where performance ended up, the supervisor always looked for and usually found something to reinforce. If performance of this individual was above the target, the statement used to reinforce that performance was something like this: "Mary, I see you have gone from 60 to 67 percent. Not only is that improvement but even greater than the target of 65 percent established yesterday. What do you think we ought to shoot for tomorrow?" On the other hand, if the performance hit the target exactly, the statement made to reinforce the job behavior went something like this: "Mary, I see that we have hit our target of 65 percent, which is an improvement of 5 percent over your performance level of (yesterday, last week, so far this week, last month, etc.). We're moving in the right direction now. What do you think we ought to set as a target for tomorrow?" Neither of these performance levels (at or above target) poses any particular problem for reinforcement techniques. However, when performance is below minimum acceptance levels, it becomes more difficult to find something to reinforce without giving the employee misinformation on his or her performance. Here is how that was done.

If performance falls between the previous level and the target level, the statement used to reinforce that movement would be: "Mary, I see that your sales results have moved from a level of 60 percent to a level of 63 percent, and I really appreciate the effort that has gone into that improvement. We are making progress and that is the most important thing as we move toward our overall target of 100 percent. What do you think would be a realistic goal to establish for tomorrow (next week, etc.)?"

When the employee merely maintains his or her previous performance level or even slips back a little, it is more difficult to find something to improve. However, it is at this performance level that the greatest effort is needed. It is the marginal performer who is most in need of help. Here is where shaping becomes most important. Shaping involves selecting successive approximations that are closer and closer to the desired result. In this case, although the results have not shown improvement, there is usually some, even if minor, improvement made on each individual sales effort. By shortening the feedback cycle to even less than one day, substantial improvements were made by employees whose performance did not immediately reflect increased efforts on their part.

Let's suppose, for example, that a service representative had a performance level of 60 percent but a consistently established target of 65 percent. By shortening the feedback cycle and backing up from overall job results to specific job behaviors (i.e., identifying for the customer the advantages of a touch-tone phone, extension in the kitchen, extension in the basement where the washer and dryer are located, etc.), the supervisor had something to reinforce. If on a particular call, the service representative did an especially good job or even improved over previous efforts, the supervisor could reinforce that behavior, thereby increasing the probability of that behavior's occurring again. As soon as the behavior occurred frequently enough, its effects would be felt in sales and sales would quickly move from 60 percent to a higher percentage. At that point, the supervisor could stop reinforcing specific behaviors and begin reinforcing increases in sales on a daily or weekly basis.

The results of these three changes—goal setting on a more frequent basis, shortened feedback cycles, and more frequent use of positive reinforcement—had immediate, substantial, and long-term impact on sales. Sales, as a percentage of opportunity to sell, went from 86 percent in January 1974 to 146 percent in January 1975. More importantly, the new level has been maintained then improved upon. Today the sales are averaging between 175 and 200 percent, and the company ranks 8 in sales out of the 19 operating companies.

WAREHOUSE MANAGEMENT

John Sweeny is the general foreman at the master distribution center for one of the major automobile manufacturers. The center covers over a million square feet of warehouse space and carries 105,000 different part numbers. Inventory runs around $50 million. Between 40,000 and 50,000 line orders are shipped each week. Each day, 300,000 pounds of material move into the warehouse and 300,000 pounds move out. John's firm is considered a well-run company and has been heavily involved in goal setting.

Several years ago, John attended a five-day workshop on the application of behavioral technology in organizations. The primary emphasis of the workshop was development of behavior-change projects that workshop participants could develop in their own organizations. John at that time had five foremen working for him and decided to include them in the development of the projects. Each afternoon at the conclusion of the workshop for that day, John went to work and reviewed the content covered during the day with his five foremen. Additionally, he spent time the following week covering the details involved in developing the project. While John was coaching his foremen in the use of these techniques, each of them was beginning the first step in the development of the project—developing baseline data. Baseline data is the performance level that existed prior to the introduction of the techniques in the organization. Several target areas were selected by John and his foremen—absenteeism, incoming loads unplaced at the end of the shift, percentage of orders picked per day, and tickets bounced (unable to fill the order) because of misplacement of parts in the bin. Absenteeism was running at approximately 9 percent. John and his foremen decided that absent employees were not of much use in meeting production targets. On the other hand, vacations were part of the union contract and had to be lived with. They therefore decided that absenteeism would include excused absences, unexcused absences, and disciplinary layoffs but not vacation time.

John and his foremen decided to concentrate on attendance—providing positive rather than negative feedback—instead of on absenteeism. Thus, the measurement system they undertook was improving attendance. Attendance stood at 91 percent. Graphs were developed for the shift as a whole and for each of the five departments within the shift. Prizes were awarded to each department depending upon attendance rate. The purpose of the prizes was to draw attention to attendance as well as to provide the basis for some additional feedback in getting the project off the ground. It was decided that everyone would get a prize but each prize was of a different value. The prizes ranged from an alarm clock to a T-shirt. Using the graph as a basis for reinforcement, John reinforced his foremen not only for improvements in their individual departments, but also for the effect their department had on the overall shift in the graph. The foremen in turn reinforced individual employees as they came to work saying things like, "James, I'm glad to see you're here today. Good attendance is important. We need you and you are an important part of the crew."

Two things are of particular note here. First, John was reinforcing each foreman and the foremen were aware that he was doing this deliberately. Many managers who examine these techniques say that if an employee knows you are using positive reinforcement, it doesn't work. That's just not so. In fact, we have often found that it works better because you are able to select those reinforcers that work for each particular individual. In talking with the foremen after the project had been underway for some time, I questioned them about this issue. Did they feel manipulated because John was using the techniques of positive reinforcement on them? The general consensus was that they were aware of what he was doing and even liked it. They admitted that their initial assumption on hearing about the techniques and how to use them was that they would lead to indecisive management. However, after John and the foremen had practiced positive reinforcement for a while and combined it whenever possible with extinction, they found the results to be extremely rewarding.

In some situations, however, workers abused the policies and it was necessary to add negative consequences for the wrong behavior, including layoffs, verbal warnings, and the like. One supervisor said he felt he was an even tougher manager than formerly; however, he said, his was a different kind of toughness. "It's a mental toughness rather than having to feel physically tough. I not only like it better, but it seems to work better besides." Thus, the general application of the technology was that people who performed (e.g., came to work on time) were reinforced for doing so. People who did not perform some of the time were ignored, and people who were habitual offenders received punishment. Very clear limits to behaviors were set up and they were then adhered to. However, it was also found that while discipline tightened up a bit because of the increased emphasis on attendance-absenteeism, positive reinforcement helped avoid the usual frictions that so easily arise when discipline is tightened.

The result of applying these techniques was an increase in attendance over a three-month period from 91 to 96.4 percent (or a decrease in absenteeism from 9 to 3.6 percent) at a time of year when attendance was usually a major problem. At the same time, attendance was running at 96.4 percent on John's afternoon shift; it was also running at 87 percent on the day shift. The same techniques were not used on the day shift, which received normal supervisory treatment. The ten-point difference in attendance had been related to a variety of factors, including the difficulty of getting to doctors and dentists, getting cars fixed, taking kids to school, among others. Many dubious managers nevertheless felt that the use of behavioral technology contributed little if any to the ten-point spread.

Then a curious thing happened. Shortly after attendance reached 96.4 percent on the afternoon shift, two of the foreman were transferred from that shift to the day shift. They then began applying the same principles of positive reinforcement of attendance in their new departments. They used only social reinforcement (e.g., "Luke, I'm glad to see that you came to work today. Good attendance is important and you are an important part of the crew. I appreciate your effort because I know it was snowing pretty hard out there this morning"). And T-shirts, clocks, or other prizes was used. In only those two departments, attendance went from 87 to 95 percent, and the only thing that differentiated those two departments from other departments was the use of behavioral technology in tackling attendance problems. In organization after organization, we are finding that the use of techniques like this work well not only for attendance but also for tardiness. One seems to interact with the other. As attendance gets better, employees start coming to work on time more frequently than before. And the reverse is also true: as tardiness is cut down, attendance seems to improve.

Other projects that John undertook and for which he and his foremen used social reinforcement but no "prizes" were in the areas described earlier—order picking, bounced tickets, and placement of incoming loads. Using a graph as a basis for reinforcement on both a departmental and shift basis, incoming loads unplaced at the end of the shift went from an average of 70 to 1 a day. Orders picked as a percentage of orders received during the day went from an average of 80 percent to an average of 100 percent; finally, the number of tickets bounced due to misplaced parts in the bin went from an average of 45 a day to an average of a little less than 5 a day.

HEALTH CARE

The hospital administrators of a 550-bed urban hospital had been concerned about the cleanliness of their hospital. Over a period of several months, they tried a variety of programs and control techniques in the housekeeping department to improve cleanliness. Each of these programs had failed, however, at least in part to a lack of support by individual employees of the department.

Thus, the problem facing the administration was not the development of a technology to improve cleanliness but rather a technology to ensure employee implementation of the improvement program. Because previous failures in improvement programs within this department had been human rather than technical, the administration decided to combine the principles of behavior technology with a series of several quality improvement programs to improve the operating efficiency of the department.

The housekeeping supervisors participated in an in-house training workshop that included new inspection techniques and higher cleanliness standards. An important part of this process was an inspection system that provided good feedback to individual divisions within the department by giving them specific information on their performance. Other programs introduced into the department had also been technically sound but had not been supported by an extensive feedback system. The second step in this program was to train supervisors in the use of positive reinforcement, something that had not been done in conjunction with the quality improvement program introduced previously. At this workshop, supervisors were trained in the techniques described in this book including the importance of feedback in general, the importance of immediate feedback, the importance of specific information in the design of feedback systems, and the avoidance of employee anxiety by using positive reinforcement.

The third step in the introduction of the program was orientation for all employees by their supervisors. At the time of the orientation, the first inspection was conducted. It showed a cleanliness level of 33 percent, far below that desired by the administration (and for that matter, by the housekeeping department). Inspections and the ratings that accompanied them were conducted by housekeeping management. Employees and supervisors in the department were encouraged to participate in the inspection of their particular areas. During the first inspection tour, each employee was reoriented to the program and the method of inspection and told the expected level of cleanliness. In subsequent tours, supervisors and employees were encouraged to inspect some of the items themselves that provided for several key ingredients. First, it insured that consistent standards were being used by inspectors, supervisors, and employees. It also reassured individual employees (who are accountable for meeting the standards) that they had input into not only the standards but the identification of performance levels that would go into reaching these standards.

As part of the feedback system, graphs and check sheets could be viewed by any employee at any time. The feedback system was sufficiently concise that supervisors were able to allow employees to reach their own conclusions about the cleanliness of their particular area. However, the feedback sheet and information was also used as a basis for positive reinforcement. Any improvement on the part of an individual division or the department as a whole was reinforced. Combined with positive reinforcement was the use of extinction for performance that was not yet up to standard. Only in situations where the danger of cross contamination, infection, or other serious implication of poor performance existed was poor performance used as a basis for discussion. Within two months, the quality ratings reached an average level of 86 percent in all areas of the hospital. For months afterward it remained high, fluctuating between 80 and 86 percent.

What portion of that improvement is due to the application of behavioral technology and what portion is due to the installation of the quality program is unclear. What is clear is that several previous attempts were made at improving quality and none of them succeeded. Moreover, none of the previous programs had combined the use of effective feedback systems with the application of positive reinforcement, both techniques being important parts of the behavioral technology that we have discussed.

Applications of this combination are not unusual in business and industry. Many organizations are finding that introduction of these changes in their technical system (e.g., industrial engineering, methods improvement, new machines, new equipment, new scheduling, etc.) is often eased when combined with techniques described in this book. Many organizations, in fact, have gone back and used the technique to reintroduce (usually successfully on reintroduction) technical systems that were unsuccessful when first tried.

RIPPLING STONE EFFECT

In the hospital, as in many other organizations, the results accomplished in the department that initially uses the techniques become widely known throughout the organization. As is usually the case, the other departments quickly become highly interested in using the techniques themselves—either in combination with some other new techniques, to introduce a new program, or simply to improve what they already have.

The hospital experienced a phenomenon that has occurred in many organizations. After the successful application of the housekeeping techniques, it was decided to expand the application of behavioral technology to supervisory personnel from other departments within the hospital. In EKG services, behavioral technology was used to improve the performance of EKG technicians in two areas: tardiness and output. Tardiness of one technician was decreased from an average of 55 minutes a week to an average of 5 minutes per week. Another technician focused on hourly output; his hourly output doubled, from 2.5 to 5 tracings per hour. This occurred in approximately two weeks.

In the dietary department, the techniques were used to reduce both minor as well as major problems. On the minor side, the frequency of the following problems diminished in an approximately two-week period:

1. Breaking dishes when unloading from carts.
2. Improper loading of dishes on a rack.
3. Allowing a machine to run out of soap.
4. Turning down water temperature.

Major problems that were tackled include total dishwashing time, tardiness, absenteeism, and punching out early. Each of these was graphed and improvements were reinforced by supervisory personnel. Over a six-week time period, the following occurred:

1. Tardiness was reduced by six man-hours per week.
2. Punching out early was reduced by one man-hour per week.
3. Absenteeism was decreased from 90 to 20 man-days per month.
4. A total reduction of three full-time positions was possible with an increase of only 15 minutes in washing time.

In a variety of organizations, the techniques of behavioral technology are being used effectively to improve employee performance. In manufacturing, health care, sales, retailing, wholesaling-distribution, government at all levels, and service organizations, behavioral technology is paying off in the form of reduced costs, absenteeism, tardiness, scrap, rejects, rework, and error rate as well as in the form of improved margins, sales, market penetration, production, order size, turnaround time, and profits.

In short, behavioral technology is a proven technique for improving employee productivity. It gives us the tools to change employee behavior in a positive manner in order to improve overall organizational performance.

BEHAVIOR CHANGE AND SELF-MANAGEMENT

In case after case, behavioral technology has helped managers improve the performance of their individual departments and the overall organization. In each situation, however, a key ingredient precedes the improvement: the manager's own behavior must change. Before John could improve the performance of his warehouse, he had to change his own behavior. Before Howard was able to save his firm $400,000 through behavior-change techniques, he had to change his own behavior. Before the hospital was able to improve performance of the dishwashing crew, its supervisors had to change their own behavior.

The use of behavioral technology in organizations can be successful if managers are willing to change their own behavior first. Behavioral technology thus becomes in a very real sense a system of self-management. It forces managers to examine performance problems and examine how their own behavior might be causing those problems—perhaps by inadvertently reinforcing the wrong behavior of employees, failing to acknowledge improvements in performance levels, mistiming reinforcement or punishment, improperly using feedback systems, or any of the slight steps we might take that would have a large impact on employee behavior.

Managers who follow the techniques described in this book will find not only does their own behavior change, but such a behavior change pays off twice—in improved employee morale and improved employee productivity. Any technique that brings about these two results should be incorporated into every manager's tool kit.

Notes

Chapter I
1. *Work in America.* Report of a Special Task Force to the Secretary of Health Education and Welfare (Cambridge, Mass.: MIT Press) 1973, p. xvi.
2. "A New Ethic for Work," Barry Posner, Alan Randolph, and Max Wortman, Jr., *Human Resource Management,* Fall 1975, p. 15.

Chapter IV
1. Data adapted from Abraham H. Maslow, *Motivation and Personality,* 2nd ed. (New York; Harper and Row, 1970), pp. 35–46.
2. J. B. Ritchie, "Today's Success, Tomorrow's Challenge: An Attitude Toward the Future," *Michigan Business Review,* May 1973, pp. 26–31.
3. For an interesting discussion of this subject, see William C. Budd, *Behavior Modification, The Scientific Way to Self Control* (Roslyn Heights, New York; Libra Publishers, 1973), pp. 24–25.

Chapter VI
1. DePhillips, Boliver, and Cribben, *Management of Training Programs* (Homewood, Ill.: Richard D. Irwin), 1960.

2. D. Philias Cole, "Measuring the Results of Supervisory Training," *Training and Development Journal,* November 1969.
3. Robert J. House, *Management Department: Design, Evaluation, and Implementation,* Bureau of Industrial Relations, Graduate School of Business Administration (Ann Arbor, Mich.:) The University of Michigan, 1967, p. 81.

Chapter VII
1. From *Praxis Reports,* Praxis Corporation, Morristown, New Jersey.
2. The entire Emery Air Freight example has been published by several sources. Three such sources are *Praxis Reports,* Praxis Corporation, Morristown, New Jersey; Edward J. Feeney Associates, Ridgefield, Connecticut; and an article by Dugan Laird in the March 1971 issue of *Training Magazine* entitled "Why Everything is All Loused Up, Really."

Chapter VIII
1. The distinction between reinforcement and feedback as well as the reason for distinguishing between them were noted by Dale Brethower in *Behavioral Analysis in Business and Industry,* 1972 published by Behaviordelia, Kalamazoo, Michigan.

Chapter XI
1. H. M. Parsons, "What Happened at Hawthorne?", *Science,* March 8, 1974, pp. 922–932.

Index

78 79 80 9 8 7 6 5 4 3 2 1